Innovation in Jewish Law

A Case Study of
Chiddush in *Havineinu*

Michael J. Broyde

URIM PUBLICATIONS
Jerusalem • New York

Innovation in Jewish Law: A Case Study of *Chiddush* in *Havineinu*
By Michael J. Broyde

Printed in Israel.
ISBN 13: 978-965-524-036-8
Urim Publications
P.O. Box 52287, Jerusalem 91521 Israel

Lambda Publishers Inc.
527 Empire Blvd., Brooklyn, New York 11225 U.S.A.
Tel: 718-972-5449 Fax: 718-972-6307, mh@ejudaica.com

www.UrimPublications.com

This book is dedicated
to the many members of the
Young Israel of Toco Hills, Atlanta
who have encouraged me to
learn, teach, observe, perform,
and fulfill the words of God's Torah
as the rabbi of our community
for fourteen years.

━━━

The book is also lovingly dedicated
to my wife Channah S. Broyde
and our children
Joshua Emanuel,
Aaron,
Rachel Irene,
and Deborah Malka,
each of whom has made me
a much better person,
in ways too complex even to list.
Without a doubt,
I would be a lesser person
but for my family.

Table of Contents

Acknowledgements
and a brief note on the intellectual history of this work

I have been using *Havineinu* as a paradigmatic text to teach about the halachic process since the founding of the Young Israel in Atlanta in August of 1994, and many members have heard many parts of this essay (some more than once). I would be remiss if I did not take this occasion to express my deep appreciation for the unparalleled opportunities the Young Israel has afforded me to publicly teach and thereby refine my thoughts on many varied matters of Torah and halacha (Jewish law). I am incredibly proud of the flourishing community we have created, with serious *tefillah* (prayer) and Torah study at its heart, and I am excited to see it move on to its next stage of growth, while retaining its core values.

Reuven Steinberg, now living in Israel, first wrote down some of my lectures on *Havineinu* as a case study for innovation in halacha more than a decade ago; Caren Torczyner (née Gottleib) edited a prior version of this work; and Deborah Loubser Kerzhner expanded it into the format in which it now appears. Akiva Berger, Michael Cinnamon, Michael Deutsch, Fruma Farkas, Daniel Goldstein, Nadav Recca, and Rabbi David Perkel all contributed significant edits and additions to this work. Michael Ausubel has edited—very well, indeed—nearly everything I have written for the past half decade and will be missed while he prospers at Columbia University School of Law. I am grateful to each of the above and many others, and I thank them wholeheartedly.

Michael J. Broyde
24 Kislev, 5770
December 11, 2009

The author would like to express his thanks to the Center for Study of Law and Religion at Emory University and the John Templeton Foundation whose support of an interdisciplinary project on The Pursuit of Happiness funded both the research and publication of this book. As the Shulchan Aruch writes (in Yoreh Deah 384:3) there is no happiness greater than innovation in Jewish law.

Preface
Innovation as a mode of change within Jewish law

One of the most controversial discussions raging in both the academic and popular discourses about Jewish law, halacha, addresses the question of how Jewish law undergoes change, if, in fact, it does. A survey of the various opinions seems to portray few options as normative. One belief is that Jewish law does not change. An opinion on the other end of the spectrum is that the rabbis can change Jewish law in well-nigh any way they wish. A third school of thought emphasizes Rabbinically enacted decrees and ordinances (*takkanot* and *gezeirot*) as modern tools of change and development within Jewish law.

In fact, while all of these approaches contain elements of truth, both as a matter of theory and as a matter of practice, none of them provides any sort of true image of how substantive Jewish law actually functions. Jewish law has been neither rigid throughout the ages, nor malleable to every desired outcome; Post-Talmudic Rabbinically-enacted decrees and ordinances have played only a minor role in amending Jewish law in the last millennium. In fact, the primary mechanism that causes change in Jewish law is not accurately described by any one of these approaches.

Jewish law's most significant form of change is innovative interpretation (*chiddush*) and represents—by far—the most frequent way in which normative Jewish law undergoes substantive development that results in new rulings and rules (which are not in fact "new" at all). Consider a parallel discussion found in secular literature: procedures to change American constitutional law. The United States Constitution is quite clear on this issue. Article V, entitled "Amendment," states:

> The Congress, whenever two thirds of both Houses shall deem it necessary, shall propose Amendments to this Constitution, or on the Application of the Legislatures of two thirds of the several States, shall call a Convention for proposing Amendments, which, in either Case, shall be valid to all Intents and Purposes, as Part of this Constitution, when ratified by the Legislatures of three fourths of the several States, or by Conventions in three fourths thereof, as the one or the other Mode of Ratification may be proposed by the Congress...

Constitutional change occurs when an amendment is proposed either by Congress or by state legislators in a constitutional convention and then ratified by the states. Although these appear to be the primary modes of change, in over two hundred years, only twenty-seven amendments to the constitution have been passed, and no constitutional conventions have been held.

While one could write a book about how the constitution changes only referring to Article V of the constitution, that book would be woefully incomplete; the vast majority of constitutional change in the United States is a result of interpretation. The Supreme Court is historically charged with interpreting the constitution, and often their understanding of this binding document changes. Unlike amendments, which change the content of the law, reinterpretation changes the application and understanding of the law.

The same concept of interpretation is true in Jewish law. The Sages of the Talmud, and their modern day heirs, are charged with the duty to study, infer, and apply halacha, answering questions of Jewish law for its adherents in every generation. Without explicitly invoking change, each scholar and each generation has an inclination to accept the validity or invalidity of particular types of arguments or particular sources. Thus, normative halacha changes continuously through the process of study and analysis. Sometimes this change is through the decision of an authority that one approach—previously thought incorrect—is in fact correct; sometimes it is through the reinterpretation of sources motivated by the search for truth; sometimes it is because economic pressures force the re-evaluation of the sources; and sometimes Jewish law responds to a new reality, as technology, society and social conditions, or scientific knowledge change.

While this fact is obvious to all who have studied halacha, it is frequently not clearly explained in the literature commenting on halacha. This phenomenon is understandable, as while incremental changes of this type are indigenous to any legal system and immediately apparent, it is not always perceptible and often misinterpreted. Some of the silence surrounding this mechanism for change comes from the fact that this type of growth cannot occur in the open, and some of the silence comes from the sense that this process will be misunderstood by some as a license for infinite growth that will come to undermine the tradition, which it certainly is not.

Rather than attempt to demonstrate this concept of legal innovation through a myriad of separate examples, each of which would have to be explained in great detail, this work seeks to examine one small area where normative practice has undergone a considerable amount of change, and yet has done so solely through the process of innovation (*chiddush*)—re-analysis of the sources. This re-analysis is not driven by one factor alone; rather, it is a combination of three activities.

I. The first avenue of change is abstract study. Jewish law requires that its adherents study Jewish law faithfully, and many great minds have devoted their whole lives to the perfection of their understanding of Jewish law. Jewish law, with its large corpus of texts and a long history of study, requires explanations and clarifications—a process which results in new interpretations. Additionally, rabbis have understood the sources differently in the abstract, leading to various interpretations of normative Jewish law. Although all *poskim* (sing., *posek*; decisors of Jewish law) have as their goal the complete understanding of a halachic concept, this end can be achieved through a variety of methods.

II. The second impetus for change is development of technology. As technology advances (or occasionally recedes), Jewish law is confronted with a variety of cases that were not addressed in the previous generation's sources. Taking the rules found in one technological setting and applying them to another setting is always very difficult. Such action is subject to disagreement about which analogies are apt and which analysis is accurate.

III. Similarly, changes in social and economic conditions are a third stimulus for reinterpretation and application of sources. As Jews move through different lands, questions arise about the application of halachic rules to new surroundings and varied cultures. The cultural diversity and wider economic opportunities encountered by the Jewish community certainly have increased in light of emancipation. Of course, the stipulations above regarding the application of rules to new technologies apply to new social and economic milieus as well.

In both the second and third types of impetus for innovation, it is not that new laws are being conceived in light of new surroundings; rather, the same system of thought and underlying concepts are being applied to a new situation. These three factors combined seem to be the catalyst for the various changes found in the area of prayer. My thesis is that these factors are the basis for change in almost every area of Jewish law.

I have written previously on this point in relation to shaving, showering, and smoking on the intermediate days of festivals (*Chol HaMo'ed*), to take but three examples of many. Technology (the second impetus) has created a halachically permissible way to shave; and for social and economic reasons (the third factors), many religious Jews choose to be clean-shaven. This has led a number of contemporary halachic authorities to reconsider the prohibition of shaving on *Chol HaMo'ed*. Likewise, two hundred years ago, most authorities permitted smoking on festivals (*Yom Tov*) because most people enjoyed smoking, which they thought was a healthy activity. In that same era, regular bathing or showering in hot water was not viewed as "of benefit to all" (*shaveh le-chol nefesh*) and was technologically difficult to do, and thus rabbinically prohibited on festivals. Today in America, smoking is viewed as hazardous and is clearly not "of benefit to all" (*shaveh le-chol nefesh*); on the other hand, daily showering is a normal activity. Consequently, normative halacha today might opt for prohibiting smoking on festivals while permitting showering.[1] As is obvious from these examples, social, technological, and economic factors are often interconnected.

The goal of this monograph is to trace the development of the halacha in one particular area: the recitation of the abstract, abridged form of *Shemoneh Esreh* commonly referred to in the rabbinic literature as *Havineinu*. In Talmudic times, the abstract *Shemoneh Esreh* apparently was recited with much greater frequency than it is in our day. Indeed, many modern prayer books (such as the ArtScroll Siddur[2]) completely leave out *Havineinu*. The following chapters will chart the halachic history of this unique prayer from beginning to end, in a variety of different lights, so as to give the reader a clear sense of how the mechanisms of change in Jewish law work in practice in this area.

Although the area of halacha addressed within this book—rules related to prayer—seems unaffected by technology, the invention of the printing press had major impact on this area. Without readily available prayer books (*siddurim*), most people had to recite prayers from memory and had to be self-sufficient in their knowledge of

---

[1] For more on this, see Michael J. Broyde, "Shaving on the Intermediate Days of the Festivals," *Journal of Halacha and Contemporary Society* 33:71–94 (1996) and Michael J. Broyde and Avi Wagner, "Halachic Responses to Sociological and Technological Change," *Journal of Halacha and Contemporary Society* 39:95–125 (2000).

[2] A widely used, comprehensive *siddur* that reflects normative rabbinic positions on practice in America.

the laws of prayer (as printed simple law codes were not wide spread either). The introduction of widespread, affordable prayer books made the prayer text more readily accessible and eliminated much of the accidental miswording in prayer. Additionally, many prayer books available today include various forms of instruction within, making the laws easier to follow.

Encountering danger is one factor that influences the modality of prayer. When in such a pressing situation, it is difficult to pray as usual. As society changes, concepts such as urgency and need, which frequently motivate lenient or strict stances in Jewish law, change along with it. In our modern Western society, where day-to-day danger typically is quite rare, one particular approach predominates, with this factor deemphasized. Yet in a different place in our own day and age, such as modern day Israel, where for the first time in modern Jewish history there is an army composed of many religiously observant Jews who encounter routine danger, there is a different emphasis.

I have chosen to survey the practice of reciting *Havineinu* for a number of reasons. First and foremost, it is clear to even the casual observer of Jewish law that a vast change has occurred from Talmudic times to the modern age in this area. Second, this topic is one without any apparent political or economic stress that might motivate unusual change; so too, it has not been a matter of Jewish–Gentile stress, which might have led to censorship and which would have made an evaluation of the sources much more difficult. Third, it is an area far removed from ideological controversy, which, given the potentially charged nature of any discussion about the process of change in Jewish law, should decrease the intensity of the heat and debate and increase the clarity of the light.

Finally, the topic of *Havineinu* is a relatively small, self-contained area of Jewish law, affording readers an opportunity to not only immerse themselves in study, but also to encounter the relevant sources with a degree of confidence and even mastery. While much of the purpose of this work is to guide the reader through these sources, additional individual study is encouraged. Understandably, there are many aspects relevant to *Havineinu* that could not be fully addressed in this book, and these omissions should not be viewed as oversights.

Although the practiced halacha of *Havineinu* is quite different now from that in the time of the Mishnah, it is difficult to identify the change in law as having occurred at any given time or place. Rather, the process is gradual; decisors of Jewish law examined the sources and interpreted them in light of their times and challenges. Their intellectual approach to Torah, their perception of their role in the chain of transmission, and their sense of truth directed that this approach be followed. I sincerely hope that readers will come away with a newfound understanding of and appreciation for the mechanisms of analysis, interpretation, and change that are central to the methodology of Jewish law.

In truth, the journey of *chiddush* cannot be described. It must be experienced. Thus, we embark.

Chapter One
Havineinu

1.1 Mishnah and Gemara (Berachot 29a)—an exploration of the concept of an abridged prayer

While *Shemoneh Esreh* was instituted by the Men of the Great Assembly as one of the central daily prayers, there are situations wherein it is difficult or impossible to recite this long text. Therefore, an abridged alternative, *Havineinu*, could be a possible substitute for fulfilling one's requirement of prayer during these difficult situations. *Havineinu*—which follows the basic outline of the full version of *Shemoneh Esreh*—and its halachic development is the focus of this work. Starting with the Mishnah as a foundation, this book is a guide through the applicable Talmudic sources and commentaries which clarify many technical questions regarding the recitation of *Havineinu*. Far beyond a simple presentation of the facts about *Havineinu*, this book will delve into the arguments and provide a glimpse into the world of halachic inquiry with an emphasis on the process of *chiddush* as the subtle mode of change within Jewish Law.

Havineinu is first introduced in the Mishnah. While raising the

question of the permissibility of praying an abridged version of
Shemoneh Esreh, the Mishnah does not discuss any other aspects of
this prayer.

משנה מסכת ברכות פרק ד משנה ג

רבן גמליאל אומר בכל יום מתפלל אדם שמונה עשרה רבי יהושע אומר
מעין שמונה עשרה ר' עקיבא אומר אם שגורה תפלתו בפיו יתפלל שמונה
עשרה ואם לאו מעין י"ח.

Mishnah, Berachot 4:3

Rabban Gamliel says: every day a person recites eighteen blessings
(*Shemoneh Esreh*). Rabbi Yehoshua says: [he recites] a condensed
version of the eighteen blessings (*Me'ein Shemoneh Esreh*); Rabbi
Akiva says: if prayer is familiar to him (literally, dwells upon his
lips), he should recite eighteen blessings; if not, [he recites] a
condensed version of the eighteen (*Me'ein Shemoneh Esreh*).

The Mishnah delineates three different policies regarding the daily
requirement of prayer.

1. Rabban Gamliel adopts a strict position: there is one way,
   or one preferable way, to fulfill the obligation of prayer—
   reciting the full text of the *Shemoneh Esreh*.

2. Rabbi Yehoshua disagrees: a condensed version (*Me'ein
   Shemoneh Esreh*) is an acceptable form of prayer.

3. Rabbi Akiva seems to adopt a middle position: though it is
   preferable to recite the full *Shemoneh Esreh*, for those who
   lack proficiency in prayer, a condensed version of *Shemoneh
   Esreh* might be appropriate.

The Mishnah has still left unanswered many questions regarding
Me'ein Shemoneh Esreh. What is the text of this abstracted prayer?
Under what circumstances may it be recited? Does it exempt one of
one's obligation to recite the full *Shemoneh Esreh*? Are there times of
the year when it may not be recited due to external technical
issues? All these issues, among others, will be clarified by the many
subsequent rabbinic commentators.

The attendant Gemara discusses what qualifies as a condensed
alternative to the *Shemoneh Esreh*.

תלמוד בבלי מסכת ברכות דף כט עמוד א

רבי יהושע אומר מעין שמנה עשרה. מאי מעין שמנה עשרה? רב אמר:
מעין כל ברכה וברכה, ושמואל אמר: הביננו ה' אלהינו לדעת דרכיך,
ומול את לבבנו ליראתך, ותסלח לנו להיות גאולים, ורחקנו ממכאובינו,
ודשננו בנאות ארצך, ונפוצותינו מארבע תקבץ, והתועים על דעתך
ישפטו, ועל הרשעים תניף ידיך, וישמחו צדיקים בבנין עירך ובתקון
היכלך ובצמיחת קרן לדוד עבדך ובעריכת נר לבן ישי משיחך, טרם נקרא
אתה תענה, ברוך אתה ה' שומע תפלה.

Babylonian Talmud, Berachot 29a
Rabbi Yehoshua says a condensed version of the eighteen (*Me'ein
Shemoneh Esreh*). What is a condensed version of the eighteen? Rav
said: a condensed version of each and every blessing. Shmuel said:
"Grant us (*Havineinu*), Lord, our God, wisdom to understand Your
ways; subject our hearts to fear You; forgive us so that we may be
redeemed; distance us from suffering; satisfy us with the products
of Your earth; gather our dispersed people from the four [corners
of the earth]. Judge those who stray from Your path; may Your
hand punish the wicked; may the righteous rejoice over the
building of Your city, the restoration of Your temple, the
flourishing dynasty of Your servant David, and the continuation of
the offspring of Your anointed, the son of Jesse. Answer us before
we call. Blessed are you, O Lord, who hears prayers."

The Gemara in Berachot 29a presents two variations of the text of
the condensed alternative to the full *Shemoneh Esreh*.
1. Rav's version of the abridgment includes shortened forms
   of each of the "eighteen" individual blessings.
2. Shmuel's formulation, which begins with the word
   "*Havineinu*," combines the basic concepts and themes of
   all of *Shemoneh Esreh*'s middle blessings of supplication
   into one catch-all blessing—*Shome'a Tefillah*.

Of these two, the Gemara never explicitly rules in favor of either
position. In the ensuing discussions, though, the Gemara
repeatedly makes reference to '*Havineinu*,' implying that
Shmuel's interpretation of the term "*Me'ein Shemoneh Esreh*" is
established as the accepted liturgy. Beit Yosef, in his commentary
on the Tur which formed the precursor to his own code of Jewish
law (Shulchan Aruch), notes that this is the clear consensus:[3]

---

[3] While the majority of commentators (including Bach, the other major
commentary on the Tur) accept *Havineinu*, there are opposing readings of

בית יוסף אורח חיים קי[:א]
ומשמע בגמרא דהלכה כשמואל דסוגיין בכוליה פירקא מדבר בהבינינו
אלמא הכי קיימא לן וכן פסקו כל הפוסקים.

Beit Yosef, Orach Chaim 110[:1]
It seems from the Gemara that the Halacha is like Shmuel, as the
discussion that follows throughout the chapter speaks of
'Havineinu'; we thus see that this is the way the law is
established. And so have all the decisors ruled.

While the Gemara in Berachot 29a clearly defines the terminology
of the Mishnah and specifies the text of *Havineinu*, it does not give
any indication of which of the three positions in the Mishnah
should be followed. May one recite a condensed version of the
Shemoneh Esreh in place of the full text? And, if so, in which
situations is this conclusion the case? The only comment shedding
light on this issue is a statement by Abaye that follows Rav and
Shmuel's dispute:

תלמוד בבלי מסכת ברכות דף כט עמוד א
לייט עלה אביי אמאן דמצלי הבינונו.

Babylonian Talmud, Berachot 29a
Abaye placed a curse upon one who recites *'Havineinu.'*

Rashi explains Abaye's curse:

רש"י מסכת ברכות דף כט עמוד א
לייט עלה אביי - לפי שמדלג הברכות וכוללן בברכה אחת.

Rashi, Berachot 29a, s.v. *layit*
Abaye placed a curse – because the person skips the blessings and
includes them [all] in one blessing.

Tosafot offer a different explanation:

תוספות מסכת ברכות דף כט עמוד א
לייט עלה אביי אמאן דמצלי *הבינונו* - והכי קיימא לן ויש ספרים דמסיק
הני מילי במתא אבל בדרך שרי כדמשמע במכילתין גבי רבי יוסי וכו'.

---

this Gemara—which consider Rav's version as accepted over Shmuel's
formulation. See Or Zarua, below p. 14, as well as Chayei Adam, below
p. 116.

Tosafot, Berachot 29a, s.v. *layit*

Abaye placed a curse upon one who recites 'Havineinu' – and this is the way [the law] is established for us. And there are some texts which conclude "this is the ruling in the cities, but on the road it is permitted," as is implied earlier in our tractate in the instance of Rabbi Yose (Berachot 3a)…

Prompted by an inconclusive ruling and an ambiguous phrase, the commentators arrive at several innovative explanations of this Gemara. The most apparent meaning of Abaye's enigmatic curse is that he condemns outright the recitation of *Havineinu*. However, some uncertainty remains in this reading. Aruch HaShulchan states the underlying question:

ערוך השלחן אורח חיים קי:ו

ואי סלקא דעתך דלא יצא לא שייך קללה בזה והוה ליה לומר דלא יצא
אלא ודאי יצא אלא לא עשה כהוגן ולפיכך קללו.

Aruch HaShulchan, Orach Chaim 110:6

For if you were to assume that [one who recites *Havineinu*] does not fulfill one's obligation [to pray], a curse is not appropriate; rather, he [Abaye] should have said that one doesn't fulfill one's obligation. Rather, [he does say] one [who recites *Havineinu*] certainly fulfills one's obligation but acted inappropriately; therefore, he placed the curse.

Aruch HaShulchan notes that not only is it important to recognize what Abaye said; it is also important to recognize what Abaye did not say. Abaye did not completely forbid the recitation of *Havineinu*. To do so, he need simply have used the term *"assur,"* the terminology of prohibition, or *"lo yatza"*—a phrase indicating that by reciting *Havineinu* one does not fulfill one's obligation of prayer. Instead, the case should be made that Abaye merely expressed a strong preference (or value judgment) against reciting a condensed version of the *Shemoneh Esreh*.

Thus, the commentators search for precisely what Abaye condemns. In this light, Rashi's comment here seems fitting and reasonable. Rashi interprets Abaye's curse within the context of the preceding debate between Rav and Shmuel. Rashi explains why Abaye cursed those who recited *Havineinu*—because it reduces all of the blessings of supplication into one, thereby diminishing the number of blessings, i.e., fewer blessings equals curse (as opposed to Rav's version, which includes all original blessings). As such, according to Abaye, Rav's fuller version would be preferable to Shmuel's more condensed version.

Or Zarua mirrors Rashi's commentary:

ספר אור זרוע ח"א - הלכות תפילה סימן צ
מיהו אם מתפלל מעין שמנה עשרה כרב כל שכן דעביד שפיר טפי דהא
אביי לייט אמאן דמצלי הבינינו.

Or Zarua, Vol. I – Laws of Prayer Ch. 90
However, if one recited Rav's condensed version of *Shemoneh Esreh* all the more so that such a person has acted properly, for Abaye cursed one who recites *Havineinu* [i.e., Shmuel's version].

Per Rashi's explanation of the reasoning behind the curse, Abaye's opinion can be understood as stern disapproval of the recitation of *Havineinu*, if not a rejection of it altogether. Other interpretations of Abaye's curse recast the view of *Havineinu* and preserve the possibility of its recitation, at least some of the time. Tosafot interpret Abaye in precisely this way. For Tosafot, Abaye's curse is relevant for only an aspect of *Havineinu*—when it is recited inappropriately. According to this line of thinking, Abaye did not allow one to recite the condensed version of *Shemoneh Esreh* when feasible to pray in full, such as in the case in a city. However, Abaye would not object to reciting *Havineinu* where circumstances necessitate praying an abbreviated version. Rashi and Tosafot argue whether Abaye's statement was referring to the text of *Havineinu* itself or the circumstances in which it was recited. According to Tosafot, traveling on the road would present sufficient cause to recite *Havineinu* and would therefore fall under the category of suitable situations. Tosafot's distinction between the person in the city and the person on the road echoes that of an earlier commentator—Rabbeinu Channanel.

ספר אור זרוע ח"א - הלכות תפילה סימן צ
פירש רבינו חננאל ואע"ג דלייט אביי אמאן דמצלי הבינינו יש מי שאומר
לכל מאן דאפשר ליה אבל מאן דטריד או בדרך לא לייט אביי:

Or Zarua, Vol. I – Laws of Prayer Ch. 90
Rabbeinu Channanel explained that even though Abaye placed a curse upon those who recite 'Havineinu,' there are those who say this [the placing of a curse] is only for one who could have [recited the entire prayer but did not]; but one who [is unable to recite the complete prayer because he] is distressed or on the road [and therefore recites Havineinu], Abaye never cursed.

Or Zarua delineates the hierarchy of what he considers to be preferable in prayer. Optimally, Shemoneh Esreh should be recited. If reciting Shemoneh Esreh is impossible, Rav's condensed version is preferable because it retains the most blessings. The least preferable alternative to Shemoneh Esreh is Shmuel's version of Havineinu because it condenses twelve (thirteen) blessings into one.

Tosafot indicate a parallel text ("implied earlier in our tractate in the instance of Rabbi Yose [Berachot 3a]") which draws a similar distinction. This parallel text compels Tosafot to narrow the scope of Abaye's curse. If Abaye's curse condemned all situations, a potential contradiction with the following story of Rabbi Yose would arise. By claiming that Abaye only talks about specific situations, Tosafot eliminates any possible conflict between the sources.

The Gemara in Berachot 3a adduces a series of rules pertaining to Havineinu from the following Aggadic narrative:

תלמוד בבלי מסכת ברכות דף ג עמוד א
תניא, אמר רבי יוסי: פעם אחת הייתי מהלך בדרך, ונכנסתי לחורבה אחת מחורבות ירושלים להתפלל. בא אליהו זכור לטוב ושמר לי על הפתח (והמתין לי) עד שסיימתי תפלתי. לאחר שסיימתי תפלתי אמר לי: שלום עליך, רבי! ואמרתי לו: שלום עליך, רבי ומורי! ואמר לי: בני, מפני מה נכנסת לחורבה זו? אמרתי לו: להתפלל. ואמר לי: היה לך להתפלל בדרך! ואמרתי לו: מתירא הייתי שמא יפסיקו בי עוברי דרכים. ואמר לי: היה לך להתפלל תפלה קצרה. באותה שעה למדתי ממנו שלשה דברים: למדתי שאין נכנסין לחורבה, ולמדתי שמתפללין בדרך, ולמדתי שהמתפלל בדרך - מתפלל תפלה קצרה.

Babylonian Talmud, Berachot 3a
It was taught—Rabbi Yose said: Once I was walking on the road

and I entered one of the ruins of Jerusalem to pray. Elijah (remembered for good) came and guarded the entrance until I concluded my prayer. Afterward, he said to me, "Peace unto you, my master." I replied, "Peace unto you, my master and teacher." He said, "My son, wherefore did you enter this ruin?" I replied, "To pray." He said, "You ought to have prayed on the road!" I replied, "I feared a passer-by would disrupt me." He said, "You ought to have prayed a shortened prayer" [here, "a shortened prayer" means *Havineinu*].[4] At that time, I learned three things from him: I learned that one does not enter a ruin, and that one prays on the road, and that one who prays on the road recites a shortened prayer.

On this story Tosafot comment:

תוספות מסכת ברכות דף ג עמוד א, ד"ה היה לך

...ואע"ג דלייט עלה אביי אמאן דמתפלל הבינינו. היינו דוקא בעיר אבל בשדה מותר.

Tosafot, Berachot 3a, s.v. *hayah lecha*
...And even though Abaye placed a curse upon one who prays 'Havineinu,' that is specifically in a city, but in a field (ba-sadeh, which can also be translated as in an open, uninhabited area) it is permitted.

The Gemara concerning the Aggadah about Rabbi Yose clearly presumes that a condensed version of *Shemoneh Esreh* is

---

[4] Here, a "shortened prayer" means *Havineinu*. As Tosafot comment:

תוספות מסכת ברכות דף ג עמוד א

היה לך להתפלל *תפלה קצרה* - לכאורה משמע שאין זה הבינינו. דהא קא בעי לקמן (דף ל.) מאי איכא בין הבינינו לתפלה קצרה. ... וגם על זה קשה דלקמן אמרינן שאין לומר תפלת של צרכי עמך אלא במקום סכנה. ורבי יוסי לא הוה במקום סכנה ... ונראה לי כפרוש הקונטרס תפלה קצרה דהכא היינו הבינינו...

Tosafot Berachot 3a, s.v. *hayah lecha*
You ought to have prayed a shortened prayer – At first glance, it sounds like this is not 'Havineinu,' as the Talmud asks later on (30a), "What is the difference between 'Havineinu' and a shortened prayer?" ... But this, too, is difficult, for later on we say that one may not recite the [shortened] prayer of "The needs of your nation are great..." unless one is in danger. And Rabbi Yose was not in danger... Therefore, it seems to me that the explanation of Rashi is correct, that the shortened prayer in our discussion here is *Havineinu*. ...

acceptable. In fact, it was required in the circumstance described. Mirroring their earlier commentary, Tosafot rightly notice that this seems at odds with Abaye's statement restricting *Havineinu*. In answering, they sustain the premise that Abaye's condemnation indeed serves to proscribe the recitation of *Havineinu* within certain circumstances. The conclusions drawn from the Rabbi Yose narrative serve to provide an example of the type of situation that would allow for the recitation of *Havineinu*. As a matter of law, then, *Havineinu* may not be said in ordinary inhabited environs, but given extenuating circumstances on the road, the condensed version may be—perhaps, ought to be—recited.

The conclusion drawn by Tosafot from this Gemara—that roads and other uninhabited locations are the factors which determine whether one is permitted to recite *Havineinu*—is derived from Abaye's invocation of a curse rather than the formal language of prohibition. While Abaye prefers that the full text should be recited whenever possible, many commentators conclude that this language of displeasure rather than impermissibility implies that he ultimately accepts *Havineinu* as a halachically valid option—within the correct context. At the same time, Tosafot view Abaye's extreme displeasure with the condensed version as functioning as a ban only in ordinary circumstances.

1.2 What falls into the category of *sha'at ha-dechak*?

The broad term for all of the situations in which *Havineinu* is permitted is *sha'at ha-dechak*. Rif is among the earlier commentators who use this term to circumscribe the recitation of *Havineinu*:

רי"ף מסכת ברכות דף יט עמוד ב
בשעת הדחק אבל שלא בשעת הדחק אין מתפלל הבינינו.

Rif, Berachot 19b (in Rif pagination)
[When is one allowed to recite *Havineinu*?] In a time of pressure (*sha'at ha-dechak*). But, if not in a time of pressure one does not recite *Havineinu*.

Rif's ruling not only reflects the technical law that *Havineinu* is only allowed to be recited during times of pressure. It also explains the nature of *Havineinu*, namely that it is not intended as a permanent substitute for *Shemoneh Esreh*. As reflected in the interpretation of Abaye's curse, ideally one must recite *Shemoneh Esreh*; however, situations arise where this option is not viable. As examples, one could be pressed for time or threatened by interruption. *Havineinu* is well suited for this purpose as a flexible prayer alternative since it is both briefer and less cumbersome to recite than *Shemoneh Esreh*.

"*Sha'at ha-dechak*" is literally translated as "a time of pressure," and it is a term used throughout Halachic literature. However, within this context—as a term specifically applied to prayer—an applicable definition of this term has not yet been established. The commentaries' conception of the situations that fit into the category of extenuating circumstance depicted by Tosafot and the Talmud, Berachot 3a, is advanced in the following section.

Havineinu's role—a brief comparison with tefillah ketzarah

The Gemara in Berachot 29a discusses a concept first introduced in the Mishnah in Berachot 4:4—"*tefillah ketzarah*," literally translated as "a short prayer."

The Mishnah introduces this prayer:

משנה מסכת ברכות פרק ד משנה ד

רבי יהושע אומר: ההולך במקום סכנה מתפלל תפלה קצרה...

Mishnah Berachot 4:4

Rabbi Yehoshua says: One who travels through a dangerous place recites a short prayer (*tefillah ketzarah*) ...

Clearly, *Havineinu* and this *tefillah ketzarah* are different. One clue to this fact is that Rabbi Yehoshua is the Tanna (sage) who introduces both of these concepts, and they are introduced separately in consecutive Mishnayot (Berachot 4:3 and 4:4 in our edition). If they were in fact the same prayer, there would be no need for two introductions—particulary by the same Sage. In addition to this reasoning to explain the Mishnah, the Gemara explicitly delineates between the two prayers:

תלמוד בבלי מסכת ברכות דף ל עמוד א

מאי איכא בין הבינו לתפלה קצרה? - הבינו - בעי לצלויי שלוש
קמייתא ושלוש בתרייתא, וכי מטי לביתיה לא בעי למהדר לצלויי;
בתפלה קצרה - לא בעי לצלויי לא שלוש קמייתא ולא שלוש בתרייתא,
וכי מטי לביתיה בעי למהדר לצלויי. והלכתא: הבינו - מעומד, תפלה
קצרה - בין מעומד בין מהלך.

Babylonian Talmud, Berachot 30a
What are the differences between *Havineinu* and the short prayer
(*tefillah ketzarah*)? *Havineinu*, one is required to recite the first three
and last three [blessings], and when one returns home, one is not
required to pray again; with the shortened prayer, one is not
required to recite either the first three or last three [blessings], but
when one returns home, one is required to go back and pray
[eighteen blessings]. *Havineinu* is said while standing in place; the
shortened prayer may be said while standing still or while
walking.

From an analysis of the differences discussed in the Gemara, the
commentators develop a more complete view of *Havineinu*.

רש"י מסכת ברכות דף ל עמוד א

וכי מטי לביתיה, בעי מהדר לצלויי - שהרי לא התפלל כלום מתפלת שמונה
עשרה.

Rashi, Berachot 30a
But when one returns home, one is required to go back and pray – for
one has not yet prayed anything of the eighteen blessings.

The Gemara enumerates the differences between *tefillah ketzarah*
and *Havineinu*. There are three primary areas of distinction, namely
whether one is required to:
1. frame the prayer with the first and last three blessings
   of the *Shemoneh Esreh*,
2. pray again upon arriving at the destination, and
3. stand in place while reciting the prayer.

The differences are summarized in Table 1.1.

While the Gemara only delineates the technical differences
between the prayers, it neglects to mention the most fundamental

Table 1.1
Differences between *Havineinu* and *tefillah ketzarah*

Difference	Havineinu	Tefillah Ketzarah
1. Include first and last three blessings of *Shemoneh Esreh* into the prayer?	YES	NO
2. Pray again upon arriving at the destination?	NO	YES[5]
3. Is one required to stand in place while reciting the prayer?	YES	NO[6]

[5] There is a basic dispute among the authorities over the nature of *tefillah ketzarah*. The Mishnah Berurah, Orach Chaim 110:13–15 as well as his Bi'ur Halacha notes ad loc., s.v. *ha-holech*, notes that *tefillah ketzarah* is not a substitute for *Shemoneh Esreh* and *Havineinu*. Rather, it is a version of *tefillat ha-derech* (the wayfarer's prayer) for circumstances of greater danger. Indeed, if one already recited *tefillat ha-derech* and then encountered danger, one need not say the *tefillah ketzarah*.

Aruch HaShulchan (Orach Chaim 110:8) disagrees. In his view, *tefillah ketzarah* is an even further condensation of *Shemoneh Esreh* than *Havineinu*. It is true that one who recites *tefillah ketzarah* is supposed to pray again when they return to the settlement and their mind calms down. However, rules Aruch HaShulchan, if the time for prayer has passed by the time the person arrives, one need not recite the next prayer twice as a make-up (*tashlumin*) for the missed prayer. In his view, *tefillah ketzarah* functions in some capacity as a substitute for *Shemoneh Esreh*, at least ex post facto (*be-de'avad*).

This dispute stems from an inherent textual ambiguity. In both the Mishnah and later Codes, *tefillah ketzarah* appears immediately after *Havineinu* and immediately before the wayfarer's prayer (*tefillat ha-derech*). How should these three prayers be categorized? Some, like Aruch HaShulchan, are inclined to read a progression from *Shemoneh Esreh* to *Havineinu* to *tefillah ketzarah*. Others, like Mishnah Berurah, understand *tefillah ketzarah* in conjunction with *tefillat ha-derech* which follows, rather than with the preceding concepts.

[6] Although some authorities maintain that one ought to stand in place if one is able; see Rambam, Hilchot Tefillah 4:19 and Shulchan Aruch, Orach Chaim 110:3.

difference between the two prayers—that *tefillah ketzarah* is said in a time of danger, while *Havineinu* is said even in a time of no danger. Tosafot note this difficulty and conclude that the Gemara does not discuss this most basic difference between the two prayers. Rather, it considers such a difference to be "given," and is therefore coming to expand on the various other, less apparent differences.

תוספות מסכת ברכות דף ל עמוד א

מאי איכא בין הביננו לתפלה קצרה - תימה לימא דאיכא ביניי[ה]ו דתפלה קצרה אינו מתפלל אלא במקום סכנה והביננו מתפלל אפילו שלא במקום סכנה? ויש לומר דהכי קא בעי מאי ביניי[ה]ו כל אחד במקומו תפלה קצרה במקום סכנה והביננו שלא במקום סכנה.

Tosafot, Berachot 30a, s.v. *mai*
What are the differences between Havineinu and the short prayer (tefillah ketzarah)? – Query: Why not say simply that the difference between them is that one may not recite the short prayer (*tefillah ketzarah*) except in case of danger, but *Havineinu* may be recited even when not in danger? We may respond that this is what the Gemara is asking: 'What are the differences [between these prayers] each in its respective circumstances—the short prayer (*tefillah ketzarah*) in a case of danger and *Havineinu* not in case of danger?'*

Until now, the commentators understood that Abaye limited the recitation of *Havineinu* to extenuating circumstances (*dechak*). Tosafot further limit that application by excluding circumstances of danger from this formulation. Thus, *Havineinu* is intended as neither the daily form of prayer nor a prayer appropriate for extreme situations.

Previously, Tosafot were quoted as allowing the recitation of *Havineinu* "in a field." While this comment does clearly specify exactly in which circumstances *Havineinu* is permissible, it only provides one example of such a circumstance. To identify which situations are permissible and which are impermissible, one must expound upon the examples in Tosafot. What set of circumstances is a "field," as opposed to a "city," meant to typify?

Elaborating on the technical differences between *Havineinu* and *tefillah ketzarah* articulated in the Gemara, Rif utilizes the term "sha'at ha-dechak" to describe those situations in which *Havineinu* would be appropriate.

רי"ף מסכת ברכות דף כ עמוד ב

שמעינן דלא מצלי איניש הבינינו אלא בשעת הדחק כגון מי שהוא מהלך במדבר וכיוצא בו:

Rif Berachot 20b (in Rif pagination)

[Rif quotes the Gemara dealing with the differences between *Havineinu* and *tefillah ketzarah*, then continues:] We deduce that one may not recite *Havineinu* except in pressured circumstances (*sha'at ha-dechak*), such as one traveling through a wilderness, and similar situations.

Rif details the limitations to the recitation of *Havineinu* to such cases as "traveling through the wilderness and *similar situations*." Thus, the broad term *sha'at ha-dechak* encapsulates a situation of extreme circumstances such as those encountered in the wild. However, this term remains loosely defined. What categorizes "similar situations" that would classify them as *sha'at ha-dechak*?

Rabbeinu Yonah focuses on the element of travel as a determinant of the ability to recite *Havineinu*. He starts with the same case of Rabbi Yose discussed in Berachot 3a and links it to the discussion regarding *Havineinu* found in Berachot 30a ("differences between *Havineinu* and the short prayer [*tefillah ketzarah*]"). From the delineation between the two prayers in relation to a "settlement," Rabbeinu Yonah derives a direct indication of the element of travel.

תלמיד רבינו יונה מסכת ברכות דף ג עמוד א

ומכאן היה למד שאין אומר הבינינו אלא בדרך שמפני שהיה בדרך אמר לו היה לך להתפלל תפלה קצרה דמשמע דאם לא היה בדרך לא היה לו להתפלל אלא תפילת י"ח שהיא ארוכה יותר ומביא עוד ראיה מדקאמר לקמן בפרק תפילת השחר מה בין הבינינו לתפלה קצרה הבינינו כי מטי ליישוב לא צריך לצלויי תפלה קצרה כי מטי לישוב צריך לצלויי דמשמע שאין אומרים הבינינו אלא בדרך:

Talmid Rabbeinu Yonah, Berachot 3a

From here [Ri Hazaken] derived that one only says *Havineinu* while on the road, for [only] because he [Rabbi Yose] was on the road, [did Elijah] say to him, "You ought to have prayed a short

prayer," which implies that had he not been on the road, he ought
to have recited the prayer of eighteen blessings, which is longer.
And he [Ri Hazaken] brings a further proof from what is stated
later in the fourth chapter of Berachot, "What are the differences
between *Havineinu* and the short prayer (*tefillah ketzarah*)?
Havineinu, when one returns to the settlement, one is not required
to pray again; the short prayer (*tefillah ketzarah*), when one returns
to settlement, one is required to pray [eighteen blessings]," which
implies that one only says *Havineinu* while on the road.

Rabbeinu Yonah explicitly states that one recites *Havineinu* while
on the road. He bases his assertion—the incorporation of travel
into the definition of *sha'at ha-dechak*—on the reference to the
difference in policy upon reaching a settlement, which implies
that these prayers are a response to the pressures of travel. The
consideration of *sha'at ha-dechak* is not in contradiction to
Tosafot's reading [the difference between city and field]. Rather,
it is a thematically linked to Tosafot's commentary.

Rosh, also defining this term, focuses on a different issue, the
Gemara's requirement to stand in place while reciting *Havineinu*.
He does not define *sha'at ha-dechak* based on external situations—
such as travel or location—but rather on the internal effects of the
environment on one's ability to pray.

רא"ש מסכת ברכות פרק ד סימן יח

הביננו מעומד תפלה קצרה אפילו מהלך ואע"ג דאמרינן לקמן גבי השכים
לצאת לדרך רבי שמעון בן אלעזר אומר בין כך ובין כך קורא קריאת
שמע ומתפלל ולא חייש לתפלה די"ח מעומד היינו טעמא כיון שהם י"ח
ברכות והיה צריך להתעכב בהן יהיה לבו טרוד מחמת העיכוב ולא יוכל
לכוין אבל הביננו אין בה אריכות דברים כל כך ויכול לכוין מעומד מהא
שמעינן דלא מצלי אינש הביננו אלא בשעת הדחק כגון המהלך במדבר
וכיוצא בו:

Rosh, Berachot 4:18

Havineinu is said while standing [still]; the shortened prayer may
be said even while walking. And even though we say later on
regarding rising early to embark on a journey [by wagon or by
boat], that Rabbi Shimon ben Elazar says: Either way, one recites
the Shema and then prays [the eighteen blessings (*Shemoneh
Esreh*)], and he is not concerned that the eighteen blessings must be
recited standing, that is because one is reciting the full eighteen

blessings and must pause significantly for them and one's heart is then pressured due to this delay, and one is therefore unable to concentrate (have *kavvanah*) [while standing for all of them], but *Havineinu* is not so long and one can concentrate (have *kavvanah*) while standing [still]. From this we deduce that one does not recite *Havineinu* except in cases of pressing need (*sha'at ha-dechak*), such as one traveling through a wilderness, and similar situations.

While under normal circumstances one should stand during *Shemoneh Esreh*, this is not the case during travel. Standing during prayer requires stopping and causes an additional delay in one's journey. These circumstances rush a person significantly and decrease one's ability to concentrate. On the other hand, because *Havineinu* is brief, the delay caused by standing and stopping to recite this prayer is less significant, and one will be able to have full concentration. In this light, the structure of *Havineinu* lends itself to increased concentration specifically in difficult situations. Thus, while *Havineinu* is not appropriate for every situation, it is suitable, even preferable, in a case of pressing need, such as traveling.

Whereas up to this point, the definition of *sha'at ha-dechak* has been limited to external and situational definitions of extenuating circumstances, Rosh introduces the related idea of *kavvanah*, intention during prayer, into the discussion. On the road, the concern for safety, fear of interruptions, and aversion towards delay would hinder concentration if one is forced to stay in a single place for the full *Shemoneh Esreh*. Due to this situation, *Havineinu* was introduced in order to make proper concentration more accessible during prayer. (See Table 1.2.)

Following a logical path, Rabbeinu Yonah's ruling seems to differ from Tosafot.

תלמיד ר' יונה דף ג עמוד ב
ונראה שאם עומד במקום שהוא טרוד וירא שיפסיקוהו או שלא יכול
להתפלל בכוונה תפילה ארוכה כל כך דאפילו בעיר מתפלל הביננו ...

Table 1.2

Conclusions drawn from the differences between *Havineinu* and
tefillah ketzarah

Difference	Havineinu	Tefillah Ketzarah	Commentaries' Deductions
Fundamental			
1. Said in a time of danger?	NO	YES	Tosafot: this is considered a "given" in the Gemara
Practical			
1. Include first and last three blessings of *Shemoneh Esreh* into the prayer?	YES	NO	[The deductions from this difference are peripheral to this study of *Havineinu*]
2. Pray again upon arriving at the destination?	NO	YES	Rabbeinu Yonah: Terminology 'Arriving at one's destination' implies that one is traveling while reciting *Havineinu*. Therefore, *Havineinu* is recited while traveling
3. Is one required to stand in place while reciting the prayer?	YES	NO	Rosh: Even when pausing one's journey and standing to pray, while reciting *Havineinu*, a brief prayer, one is able to concentrate. Therefore, *Havineinu* is recited in situations where one's *kavvanah* is decreased

Talmid Rabbeinu Yonah, Berachot 3b
It seems that if one is standing in a place where one is burdened
(*tarud*) and afraid of being disrupted, or one is unable to pray
attentively such a long prayer, then even in the city one is
[permitted] to recite *Havineinu*...

Rabbeinu Yonah takes Rif's statement (regarding *sha'at ha-dechak*)
to its logical extension, stating that *Havineinu* is not restricted to
cases of travel. Rather, it is appropriate for any case of pressing
circumstances, even within the more secure city. In comparison,

this ruling contradicts Tosafot, who rule that *Havineinu* is not to be recited inside a city. By following the progression of ideas in rabbinic literature, we see that these commentaries are all addressing the same issue of *dechak* even as their interpretations lead to divergent conclusions in practice.

Magen Avraham in the name of Kenesset HaGedolah, distinguishes between the situation of *dechak* identified by Rabbeinu Yonah, namely, pressure caused because one is "afraid of being disrupted," and a second, more pressing, situation of *dechak*. Significantly, his commentary is innovative in that it takes into account factors which are neither situational (such as traveling or potential interruption) nor internal (such as a lack of *kavvanah*) but time related:

מגן אברהם אורח חיים סימן קי סעיף א
בשעת הדחק - או שהשעה עוברת [כ"ה].

Magen Avraham, Orach Chaim 110:1
In sha'at ha-dechak – or that time is passing (Kenesset HaGedolah).

Rabbi Akiva Eiger adds to Magen Avraham:

הגהות רבי עקיבא איגר אורח חיים קי:א
אבל בדחק שמזכיר המג"א בריש הסימן או השעה עוברת, י"ל דבזה במוצאי שבת ויום טוב מוטב שיתפלל הבינונו ולא יזכיר הבדלה, ממה שלא יתפלל כלל.

R. Akiva Eiger, Hagahot R. Akiva Eiger, Orach Chaim 110:1
However, in the case of *dechak* mentioned by the Magen Avraham at the beginning of §110, "or when the time for prayer is about to run out [so that one is faced with a choice of *Havineinu* or nothing, rather than *Havineinu* or the full *Shemoneh Esreh*]," one might say that in this instance, at the conclusion of Shabbat or festivals it is better to recite *Havineinu* and not mention *Havdalah* [in that prayer] than not to pray at all.

According to Magen Avraham, one may recite *Havineinu* even when the *dechak* is merely time pressure. Rabbi Akiva Eiger explains and adds that were this the circumstance for an individual after Shabbat or festivals, then it would be better to recite *Havineinu* instead of not praying at all, seemingly because given the options of praying something in a sub-optimal way and not praying at all, praying—albeit in a less-than-ideal manner—is preferable, even if this means omitting *Havdalah*. In this line of reasoning, *dechak* has now been expanded to include time pressure.

Chayei Adam applies *dechak* to an auxiliary situation—an ill individual. Like a person traveling, one who lacks *kavvanah*, or one who is under time constraints, an ill individual has difficulty reciting a full *Shemoneh Esreh*.

חיי אדם כלל כד הלכות תפלה סעיף לא
בשעת הדחק – כגון שהוא בדרך במקום שירא שיפסיקוהו עוברי דרכים או שירא שיעבור זמן תפלה או חולה, מתפלל ג' ראשונות ואח"כ אומר מעין י"ח והיינו שאומר נוסח זה, הבינינו ה' אלהינו...

Chayei Adam, Laws of Prayer 24:31
In a time of pressing need – e.g., one is traveling in a place where one is afraid one will be interrupted by passersby, or one is afraid that the time for prayer will pass, or one is ill—one recites the first three blessings and then says an abstraction of *Shemoneh Esreh*, namely the following text: Grant us, Lord, our God (*Havineinu*)…

Although the commentators are building on each other's explanations and expanding the definitions of terms, fundamentally, the opinions presented in this section reflect a similar attitude to the subject matter. Along these lines, Kessef Mishneh posits that many of these commentaries are ultimately in agreement:

כסף משנה הלכות תפילה ב:ג
וכתב הר' מנוח ואע"ג דלייט אביי אמאן דמצלי הבינינו במתא מאי מתא כעין מתא דמסתמא אינו טרוד כל כך אבל אם היה טרוד מותר וכן הסכים גאון וכן כתבו הרי"ף והרא"ש וה"ר יונה.

Kessef Mishneh, Laws of Prayer 2:3
Rabbeinu Manoach wrote, "Even though Abaye placed a curse upon those who recite *Havineinu* in a city—what is a city: that [circumstance] which resembles a city, where presumably one is not burdened too greatly. However, if one was indeed burdened,

it is permitted [to recite *Havineinu*]." So agreed Gaon, and so wrote
the Rif and the Rosh and Rabbeinu Yonah.

Summary

Though use of the term *sha'at ha-dechak* has progressed toward a
unified meaning, specific applications of the concept vary. This
difference in codification could be viewed in one of two ways.
One possibility is that each commentator spelled out all the
circumstances under which one would be permitted to recite
Havineinu, and any cases not mentioned were intentionally
excluded. Alternatively, one could understand that commentators
mentioned specific situations simply to provide examples of what
is to be considered *dechak,* thus allowing for more expansive use
of *Havineinu.* The range of ideas includes Tosafot's opinion that
Havineinu should be recited "on the road" and "in the field," Rif's
introduction of the term *"sha'at ha-dechak,"* Rabbeinu Yonah's
elaboration of travel, Rosh's addition of *kavvanah,* and Chayei
Adam's inclusion of one who is ill.

These definitions are thematically related; however, upon
considered analysis, the differences between them become evident.
Although united by an underlying reasoning—the concern that
someone will come to be interrupted—Tosafot limits *Havineinu* to
locations outside the city, which commentators interpret as any
situation of trouble, and Rabbeinu Yonah has come to say
Havineinu is permitted even in a city (under circumstances of
pressure). Magen Avraham views pressure to come as a result of
time constraints, which is neither situational nor internal. Chayei
Adam also advances a *chiddush* by applying the concept of *dechak* to
an ill individual, where the situation cannot be classified as external
"pressure." (See Table 1.3.)

At this point the commentators on the Gemara have clearly
established the principle that *Havineinu* is permitted only in
circumstances of *sha'at ha-dechak.*

Though it remains unclear which of the three opinions in the
Mishnah—that of Rabban Gamliel, Rabbi Yehoshua, or Rabbi
Akiva—this position is according to, it is firmly established that

Table 1.3
Under what conditions one recites *Havineinu* — survey of various opinions (limitations/expansions)

Rif: introduces term *"sha'at ha-dechak"*
Tosafot: it is dependent on location—not recited in a city
Rabbeinu Yonah: it is dependent on action—only recited in travel or under any burden of disruption
Rosh: it is dependant on internal concerns—*kavvanah*
Magen Avraham: when the time to pray is almost ending
Chayei Adam: when an individual is ill

sha'at ha-dechak is the only distinguishing factor between various cases. Because commentators incorporate different sources into their discussions, it is important to keep in mind the explanations and conclusion of this Gemara in Berachot 29a within the context of the study of the following Gemara, Berachot 16a.

1.3 Berachot 16a: Laborers and *Havineinu*— a resolution of conflicting Baraitot

Earlier in this tractate there is another case involving *Havineinu*: a passage where the ruling regarding the ability to recite *Havineinu* appears to be more explicit. Ostensibly, this Gemara, Berachot 16a, deals with various types of laborers and their obligation to recite a full *Shemoneh Esreh,* but it does not deal with *sha'at ha-dechak*. Like the previously cited Gemara (Berachot 29a), this section focuses on developing a legal reasoning and decision based on the original Mishnah, Berachot 4:4. In addition to considering this Mishnah, the argument concerns two conflicting Baraitot followed by a third Baraita, the function of which is disputed among commentators.

תלמוד בבלי מסכת ברכות דף טז עמוד א

תנו רבנן: הפועלים שהיו עושין מלאכה אצל בעל הבית - קורין קריאת שמע ומברכין לפניה ולאחריה, ואוכלין פתן ומברכין לפניה ולאחריה, ומתפללין תפלה של שמונה עשרה אבל אין יורדין לפני התיבה ואין נושאין כפיהם. והתניא: מעין שמונה עשרה!—אמר רב ששת, לא קשיא: הא - רבן גמליאל, הא רבי יהושע. - אי רבי יהושע, מאי איריא פועלים,

אפילו כל אדם נמי! - אלא, אידי ואידי רבן גמליאל, ולא קשיא: כאן -
בעושין בשכרן, כאן - בעושין בסעודתן. והתניא: הפועלים שהיו עושים
מלאכה אצל בעל הבית קורין קריאת שמע ומתפללין, ואוכלין פתן ואין
מברכים לפניה, אבל מברכין לאחריה שתים, כיצד - ברכה ראשונה
כתקונה, שניה - פותח בברכת הארץ וכוללין בונה ירושלים בברכת
הארץ; במה דברים אמורים - בעושין בשכרן, אבל עושין בסעודתן או
שהיה בעל הבית מיסב עמהן - מברכין כתיקונה.

Babylonian Talmud, Berachot 16a

[Baraita 1] The Rabbis taught: Laborers who work for the landlord recite the Shema and the blessings before and after, eat their bread and say the blessings before and after, and recite the prayer of the [full] eighteen blessings (*Shemoneh Esreh*); but they do not descend before the ark [to lead prayers], nor do they offer the Priestly Blessings.

[Baraita 2] But does another Baraita not teach [that laborers recite] a condensed version of the *Shemoneh Esreh*?

[Discussion] Rav Sheshet said: This is no difficulty–[the first statement reflects the opinion of] Rabban Gamliel and [the second reflects that of] Rabbi Yehoshua. If so, according to Rabbi Yehoshua, why does the Baraita restrict the recitation of a condensed eighteen blessings to laborers? It should be the case for all people!

Rather, [both statements] are the opinion of Rabban Gamliel, and there is no difficulty—[the second statement applies to] wage laborers, and [the first applies to] those who work only for their meals.

[Baraita 3] And another Baraita teaches: Laborers who work for the landlord recite the Shema, pray, and eat their bread but do not recite a blessing before, and [only recite] two [blessings] after. How so? [They recite] the first blessing as usual; the second begins with the land and includes rebuilding Jerusalem. When is this the case? With wage laborers; but if they work only for their meals or if the landlord is dining with them, they bless as usual.

Rashi and Tosafot elaborate on this Gemara:

רש"י מסכת ברכות דף טז עמוד א

קורין את שמע ומברכין לפניה ולאחריה - כתקונה, וכן בזמן תפלה.
אבל אין יורדין לפני התיבה - אינן רשאין ליבטל ממלאכתן ולירד לפני
התיבה לעשות שליח צבור, שיש שם בטול מלאכה יותר מדאי.
מעין שמונה עשרה - הבינונו לדעת דרכיך כו' שכולל אחת עשרה ברכות
בברכה אחת, ושלוש ראשונות ושלוש אחרונות כהלכתן.

הא רבן גמליאל הא רבי יהושע - דתנן בפרק תפלת השחר (דף כ"ח, ב'):
רבן גמליאל אומר בכל יום ויום מתפלל אדם שמונה עשרה ברכות,
רבי יהושע אומר מעין שמונה עשרה.
עושין בשכרן - שנוטלין שכר פעולתן לבד סעודתן - צריכין למהר
המלאכה ומתפללין מעין שמונה עשרה.
אבל עושין בסעודתן - בשביל האכילה לבדה מתפללין שמונה עשרה.
והתניא - בניחותא, דיש חלוק בין עושין בשכרן לעושין בסעודתן.
ואין מברכין לפניה - שאינה מן התורה.
אבל מברכין לאחריה - שהיא מן התורה, דכתיב ואכלת ושבעת וברכת
(לקמן: ברכות מ"ח, ב')
וכוללין - שני ברכות באחת, שברכת הארץ ובנין ירושלים דומות.

Rashi, Berachot 16a

Recite the Shema and the blessings before and after – as properly established, and so too at the time for prayer.

But they do not descend before the ark – they are not permitted to be idle from their work and descend before the ark to serve as the representative of the congregation, as that would involve setting aside work for an exceeding amount of time.

A condensed version of the Shemoneh Esreh – "Grant us wisdom to understand your ways..." (*Havineinu*), which combines eleven [other] blessings into one, plus the first three and last three.

[the first Baraita reflects the opinion of] Rabban Gamliel and [the second Baraita reflects that of] Rabbi Yehoshua – as the Mishnah states (Berachot 28b) Rabban Gamliel says: every day a person recites eighteen blessings (*Shemoneh Esreh*). Rabbi Yehoshua says: a condensed version of the eighteen blessings.

Wage laborers – who earn wages from their work apart from their meals – must work quickly [and diligently] and [thus] recite a condensed eighteen blessings.

But those who work only for their meals – for the meals alone, they may recite a full eighteen blessings

And another Baraita teaches – gently (i.e., read this phrase without the inflection of a question); [this Baraita demonstrates] that a distinction exists between wage laborers and those who work only for their meals.

Do not recite a blessing before – for it is not a Torah obligation.

But they do recite [only two] blessings after – for this is a Torah obligation, as is written, "And you shall eat and be satisfied, and bless." (Below, Berachot 48b [citing Deut. 8:10]).

And includes – two blessings in one, for the blessing of the land

and that of rebuilding Jerusalem are similar.

תוספות מסכת ברכות דף טז עמוד א

אפילו כל אדם נמי – ואי תימא הא שאר כל אדם רשות ופועלים חובה.
ויש לומר דפשיטא ליה כיון שיכול לומר מעין י"ח אין זה שום חדוש אם
הפועלים אומרים אפילו לכתחלה.

Tosafot, Berachot 16a, s.v. *afilu*

It should be the case for all people – One might suggest [an alternative
answer to the Gemara's question] that for all other people [saying
a condensed version of the *Shemoneh Esreh*] is optional, but for
laborers it is obligatory. One may respond by saying that it is
obvious to [the Gemara] that since [according to Rabbi Yehoshua]
anyone may say a condensed version of the *Shemoneh Esreh*, there
is no novelty in positing that laborers [also] recite such a version
even *ab initio* (*lechatchilah*) [and not only *ex post facto* (*be-de'avad*), or
in extenuating circumstances—this is already evident and thus no
novelty].

Berachot 16a—outline of the Talmudic passage in brief

The Gemara presents two Baraitot which seem at odds with one
another. Whereas the first Baraita indicates that laborers recite a
full *Shemoneh Esreh* (without involving themselves in the communal
aspects of prayer), the second Baraita states that laborers recite
Me'ein Shemoneh Esreh—an abridged version of *Shemoneh Esreh*.
Two resolutions to this contradiction are offered in the Gemara (as
outlined in Table 1.4). Rav Sheshet suggests that the first Baraita
follows Rabban Gamliel's approach and the second follows Rabbi
Yehoshua's approach. Tosafot (above) elaborate on the Gemara's
rejection of Rav Sheshet's explanation. They question the validity of
attributing the second Baraita to Rabbi Yehoshua. If Rabbi
Yehoshua's position on the validity of an abridged version of
Shemoneh Esreh is already obvious—that he allows all people to
recite the abridged version—there is "no novelty in positing that
the laborers [in addition to everyone else] recite such a version
(*Havineinu*)." Supporting Tosafot's assertion that this resolution is
rejected, a second possibility is raised wherein the Gemara
ostensibly excludes Rabbi Yehoshua's position. This anonymous
opinion attributes both Baraitot to Rabban Gamliel—claiming that
each Baraita applies to a different case. Within his broad opinion

Table 1.4
Content of Berachot 16a

Baraita	Summary	Which opinion the Baraitot follow:	
		First Resolution (Rav Sheshet)	Second Resolution (anonymous)
Baraita #1	Laborer recites a full version, but is not involved in communal aspects of prayer	Rabban Gamliel (who said to always pray full *Shemoneh Esreh*)	Rabban Gamliel (who said to always pray full *Shemoneh Esreh*) in case of those paid in food
Baraita #2	Not full, rather *Me'ein Shemoneh Esreh* is said by laborer	Rabbi Yehoshua (who said to pray an abridged version)	Rabban Gamliel (who said to always pray full *Shemoneh Esreh*) in case of wage earners *Note: this is an exception to his general principle*
Baraita #3	In case of Grace after Meals, distinction is drawn between types of laborers: wage earner says abridged version		

concerning *Shemoneh Esreh*, Rabban Gamliel draws a distinction between the types of laborers based on the type of compensation the laborer receives, as explained by Rashi (above). If the laborer earns wages (in addition to food), he obviously is under more obligations to the land owner than a laborer who works only for food. Because he is under more pressure, he needs to recite an abridged version. The function and content of the third Baraita will be discussed in the following sections.

Rashi's approach — theft and the third Baraita's precedent

According to many commentators, including Rashi (cited above), the distinction between types of laborers drawn in the second resolution is based upon a type of theft from the employer that occurs when a laborer attends to his or her own needs—in this case prayer—while on the employer's time. According to Rashi's reading of the text, this concern for preventing theft of time only exists in the case of a wage earner but is not a concern about the food earner who is under fewer obligations to the employer. Therefore, because the individual who works for wages "must hurry to work," he must "recite a condensed eighteen blessings," and it would be unethical business practice to do otherwise. Taking more than the minimal amount of time to fulfill religious obligations amounts to theft.

Rashi explains the underlying rationale behind the seemingly arbitrary distinction drawn between different types of laborers as applied to *Havineinu*. The third Baraita draws the same distinction between laborers and thereby supports the Gemara's distinction. Following the precedent of the case of Grace after Meals in this Baraita, a distinction can be made between the wage earner and the food earner in respect to the type of prayer each should recite.

Not all commentators agree with Rashi's understanding of the function of the third Baraita. These authorities—most notably the Rif and Rosh (whose positions are described below, beginning on page 38)—believe that the Baraita serves to detract from, not support, the Gemara's second resolution. In their view, the third Baraita stands in contradiction to the first two. Indeed, the third Baraita limits the situations in which a distinction can be drawn between types of laborers solely to a case of Grace after Meals, but not any other situation. The Baraita begins "Laborers who work for the landlord recite the Shema, [and] pray." Only after this general guideline for action, which makes no mention of *Havineinu*, does the Baraita make a distinction between types of laborers—and even then it is only in regard to Grace after Meals. Other later authorities take a different perspective, explaining that the theft-based distinction drawn by Rashi was not alluded to in the Gemara Berachot 29a and is therefore invalid as its own factor. The commentators notice this discrepancy—"theft" versus "*dechak*" as criteria to recite *Havineinu*—but disagree regarding the resolution of the contradiction.

There appears to be a dramatic shift between the two concepts of *Havineinu* presented within the Gemarot—one focusing on *sha'at ha-dechak* and the other on laborers' obligations to their employer. Additionally, although one's initial impression is that this Gemara does not have any internal contradictions that need to be resolved, this is not necessarily the case. The commentators' resolutions to these internal discrepancies help to bridge the gap between the two incongruous concepts of *Havineinu* and thereby provide a more cohesive and complete concept of the *Havineinu* prayer.

Combining the two Gemarot — incorporating sha'at ha-dechak

Until now, we have portrayed the distinctions drawn by the two Gemarot as different and divergent: one makes a distinction solely based on *sha'at ha-dechak*, the other based on a laborer's obligation to manage their time ethically. In this section, the commentators bring the two sources together and use each to re-evaluate the other to bring a more comprehensive, holistic view of the institution of *Havineinu*.

In Rambam's ruling, he seems to omit *sha'at ha-dechak* as a factor of reciting *Havineinu*. He does, however, accept the distinction, established in the third Baraita in Berachot 16a, between those working only for sustenance and those working for additional wages.

רמב"ם הלכות תפילה ונשיאת כפים פרק ה הלכה ח
האומנין שהיו עושין מלאכה בראש האילן או בראש הנדבך או בראש
הכותל והגיע זמן תפלה יורדין למטה ומתפללין וחוזרין למלאכתן, ואם
היו בראש הזית או בראש התאנה מתפללין במקומן מפני שטרחן מרובה,
ומה הן מתפללין אם היו עושין בסעודתן בלבד מתפללין שלש תפלות של
תשעה עשר ברכות, היו עושין בשכרן מתפללין הביננו ובין כך ובין כך
אין יורדין לפני התיבה ואין נושאין את כפיהן.

Rambam, Laws of Prayer 5:8
Craftspersons who were working atop a tree or a scaffolding or a wall at the time for prayer descend, pray, and return to their labor; but if they were atop an olive tree or fig tree, they pray in place, as their effort [to climb down from the tree in order to pray] is great.

What do they pray? If they work only for their meals, they recite three prayers of nineteen blessings (*Shemoneh Esreh*) [over the course of the day]; those who earn wages recite '*Havineinu*.' In either case, they may not descend before the ark [to lead prayers], nor offer the Priestly Blessings.

It seems that Rambam is following Rashi's theft-based distinction. Rambam rules that certain prayers are appropriate for people based on how they are compensated for their labor. Although Rambam appears to summarize the conclusion reached by the Gemara, his formulation raises many questions. Because Rambam does not directly take into account the concept of *sha'at ha-dechak* established in the Gemara Berachot 29a, Tur, like many other commentators, questions Rambam's reading of Berachot 16a. Tur injects his own reasoning in order to account for Rambam's ruling. He attributes Rambam's distinction not only to a difference between laborers' obligation to their employers, but also to a difference between laborers based on the presence of *sha'at ha-dechak*.

טור אורח חיים סימן קי[:ב]

כתב הרמב"ם הפועלים שעושין מלאכה אצל בעל הבית מתפללין הבינינו אם עושין בשכרן שנוטלין שכר פעולתן לבד מסעודתן שאז צריכין למהר למלאכה אבל אם אין נותן להם שכר אלא שעושין בשכר הסעודה מתפללין כל שמונה עשרה אבל אין יורדין לפני התיבה ואין נושאין כפיהן ואפשר שחושב פועלים כשעת הדחק.

Tur, Orach Chaim 110[:2]

The Rambam wrote that laborers who work for the landlord recite '*Havineinu*' if they work for wages—that is, they earn wages apart from meals—for then they must hurry to go about their work; but if they receive no wages other than meals, they recite the entire *Shemoneh Esreh*, but they nonetheless may not descend before the ark [to lead prayers], nor offer the Priestly Blessings—and it is possible that he [Rambam] considers laborers to be a case of emergent need (*sha'at ha-dechak*).

Notice Tur's interesting language, "and it is possible that he [Rambam] considers..." He seems to postulate about Rambam's motivation rather than state an authoritative fact. Tur seems to try to find a way to include the concept of *sha'at ha-dechak* into

Rambam's formulation—noting that a wage laborer has to "hurry to go about their work." Beit Yosef is perplexed by Tur's attribution of the halacha, leading him to reattribute the halacha to the Gemara. Notably, he does not change the Tur's formulation, which suggests that he agrees with it.

בית יוסף אורח חיים סימן קין[:ב]

דברי הרמב"ם הם בפרק ה' מהלכות תפילה (הלכה ח') ומלשון רבינו
נראה שהוא סבור שהם דברי עצמו ואינו כן אלא תלמוד ערוך הוא בפרק
היה קורא (טז.)...

Beit Yosef, Orach Chaim 110[:2]
This citation of the Rambam appears in Hilchot Tefillah 5[:8]. From the language of our master [the Tur], it seems that he is of the opinion that these [words] are Rambam's own innovation. But it is not so; rather, [what Rambam says] is a set passage in the Talmud (Berachot 16a)...

Tur's presentation is not exactly in line with the simple reading of the Gemara. Tur adds two points that subtly shift the issue of the laborers from the principle of theft, established in the current Gemara (Berachot 16a), to that of *dechak* (from Berachot 29a):

1. He justifies the distinction drawn by the Gemara and the Rambam based not on the laborers' distinct obligations to their employer, but on how these increased obligations result in wage laborers facing more pressure in their work.
2. He concludes with the statement that laborers, due to this added pressure, may be considered in *sha'at ha-dechak*.

In his unique formulation, Tur establishes a concrete link between the two Gemarot. He applies the conclusion of Gemara 29a to the reading of Gemara 16a—an obvious *chiddush*. In order to elaborate on and clarify the nature of this connection, several commentaries on Tur's reading will be presented. They all incorporate rulings from Berachot 29a into their interpretation. Additionally, they specify which of the positions in the Mishnah—those of Rabban Gamliel, Rabbi Yehoshua, or Rabbi Akiva—they believe the halacha to be in accordance with.

A different approach — *All laborers recite a full* Shemoneh Esreh

Rif and Rosh's approach to this Gemara provides a basis for many of the commentaries on Tur's reading of Rambam. Unlike Rambam, Rif and Rosh's glosses on the Gemara only cite the third Baraita as halacha, omitting any distinction between laborers with regard to *Shemoneh Esreh*:

רי"ף מסכת ברכות דף ט עמוד ב

תנו רבנן הפועלין שהיו עושין מלאכה אצל בעל הבית קורין קריאת שמע ומתפללין ואוכלין פתן ומברכין לפניה ולאחריה שתי ברכות כיצד ברכה ראשונה כתקנה שניה פותח ברכת הארץ וכולל לבונה ירושלים בברכת הארץ וחותם בברכת הארץ במה דברים אמורים כשעושין בשכרן אבל בעושין בסעודתן או שהיה בעל הבית מסב עמהם מברכין כתקנן ארבע:

Rif, Berachot (9b in Rif pagination)

The Rabbis taught: Laborers who work for the landlord recite the Shema, pray, eat their bread, and recite the blessing before and [only] two blessings after. How so? [They recite] the first blessing as usual; the second begins with the land, includes rebuilding Jerusalem, and is concluded with the blessing of the land. When is this the case? With wage laborers; but with those who work only for their meals or if the landlord is dining with them, they bless four [blessings] as usual.

רא"ש מסכת ברכות פרק ב סימן יד

תנו רבנן הפועלים שהיו עושין מלאכה אצל בעל הבית קורין קריאת שמע ומתפללין בכל יום ג' פעמים י"ח. ואוכלין פתן ומברכין לפניה ומברכין לאחריה שתי ברכות. כיצד ברכה ראשונה כתקנה. שניה פותח בברכת הארץ וכולל בונה ירושלים בברכת הארץ. במה דברים אמורים בעושין בשכרן אבל עושין בסעודה או שהיה בעל הבית מיסב עמהם מברכים כתקנה ד':

Rosh, Berachot 2:14

The Rabbis taught: Laborers who work for the landlord recite the Shema and pray three times *eighteen [blessings] daily* [emphasis added], eat their bread and recite the blessing before and [only] two blessings after. How so? [They recite] the first blessing as usual; the second begins with the land and includes rebuilding Jerusalem. When is this the case? With wage laborers; but those who work only for their meals or if the landlord is dining with them, they bless four [blessings] as usual.

In their presentations of the issue, both Rif and Rosh merely quote the third Baraita of the Gemara, evidence that they do not consider the first two Baraitot to be in accordance with the final halachic ruling. Rosh's writing is explicit: he cites a version of the Baraita that unequivocally rules that *Shemoneh Esreh* is an essential prayer for all laborers. Rosh specifically rules against the second resolution between the Baraitot by stating that one must recite the full *Shemoneh Esreh* three times daily in every situation, meaning that no group has *carte blanche* to recite *Havineinu* daily.

The next chapter will explore how two post-medieval commentators on the Codes of Jewish law re-examine these sources to reach a different conclusion.

Chapter Two
Havineinu II
Bach, Taz, and a re-examination of the sources

2.1 Reassessing Berachot 16a

Until this point, we have essentially explored *Havineinu* solely through the Gemara and Rishonim. This chapter explores how the intellectual dialogue between Bach and Taz—father- and son-in-law—writing on the Tur and Shulchan Aruch in the sixteenth and seventeenth centuries respectively, refines our understanding of the Talmudic text, innovates within that text, and ultimately forces a re-examination of the Talmudic sources and Rishonim. The final section revisits the question of which Tanna's view is accepted in our central Mishnah: Rabban Gamliel, Rabbi Yehoshua, or Rabbi Akiva.

Bach's explanation of Tur – the function of the third Baraita

There are several commentaries who do not view the third Baraita to be functioning as a support of the distinction made between laborers. Agreeing with these commentaries' premise, Bach contends that Tur's presentation is not an oversight, but a carefully constructed formulation which comes to account for the contradiction between Rambam's position and that of Rif and Rosh.

ב"ח אורח חיים קי:ד

כתב הרמב"ם הפועלים וכו' ואפשר שחושב פועלים כשעת הדחק- תימה
הלא תלמוד ערוך הוא כדברי הרמב"ם בפרק היה קורא (דף ט"ז עמוד א)
ומביאו בית יוסף ואם כן מאי קאמר רבינו עלה דהרמב"ם ואפשר דחושב
פועלים כשעת הדחק דאין הרמב"ם חושב כלום מדעתו דאינו כותב אלא
מה שעולה מן הסוגיא. ונראה דדעת רבינו כיון דהאלפסי (דף ט עמוד ב)
והרא"ש (פ"ב סי' יד) לא פסקו כי הך אוקימתא דמחלק לענין תפילת י"ח
בין עושין בשכרן דמתפללין הבינונו ובין עושין בסעודתן דמתפללין י"ח
ולא הביאו אלא הברייתא כצורתה וזה לשונה הפועלים שעושין מלאכה
אצל בעל הבית קורין קריאת שמע ומתפללין ואוכלין פתן ואין מברכין
לפניה אבל מברכין לאחריה שתים כיצד ברכה ראשונה כתיקונה וכו' במה
דברים אמורים בעושין בשכרן אבל עושין בסעודתן או שהיה בעל הבית
מיסב עמהם מברכין כתיקונה. אלמא דאין מחלק בין עושין בשכרן וכו'
אלא לענין ברכת המזון אבל בתפילה אין חילוק דבכל ענין חייבין
להתפלל י"ח כדקתני ברישא בסתם וקורין קריאת שמע ומתפללין דלא
משמע אלא תפילה גמורה של י"ח והרא"ש נמי דקדק עוד לפרש כשכתב
ברייתא זו דכתב בה ומתפללין בכל יום שלש פעמים י"ח ואוכלין פתן
וכו'...

Bach, Orach Chaim 110:4

[Quotes Tur's suggestion that Rambam bases his halacha on *sha'at ha-dechak*.] Query: Are these words of the Rambam not in accord with a set passage in the Talmud in the second chapter of Berachot (16a), and which is cited by Beit Yosef?! If so, why does our master [Tur] say about the Rambam that it is possible that he considers laborers to be a case of pressing need (*sha'at ha-dechak*)? The Rambam does not conjure up anything simply of his own accord; he merely writes that which emerges from the Talmudic passage(s)! It appears that the view of our master emerges from the fact that the Rif and the Rosh did not rule in accordance with the answer with regard to the full eighteen blessings that distinguishes between wage laborers who recite *Havineinu* and those who work only for their meals who recite the [full] eighteen blessings (*Shemoneh Esreh*), and only cite the [third] Baraita in its original form as follows: "Laborers who work for the landlord recite the Shema, pray, and eat their bread and do not recite a blessing before, but recite [only] two blessings after. How so? The first blessing as usual … When is this the case? With wage laborers; but those who work only for their meals or if the landlord is dining with them, they bless as usual." We see from this that it only distinguishes between wage laborers, etc. for the Grace after Meals, but for prayer there is no distinction made: in all circumstances [laborers] are required to recite the [full] eighteen blessings, as the first part of the Baraita says simply "Recite the Shema and pray," which implies a full prayer of eighteen blessings. And the Rosh was even more exacting to explain this when he recorded this Baraita, for he wrote "...and pray three times eighteen blessings daily, eat their bread..." (Continued below)

Bach contends that the Gemara ostensibly rejects applying a distinction between laborers as a resolution of the contradiction between the Baraitot. Thus, the second reasoning (which attributes the difference between Baraitot to a difference in laborers) posited by Rashi, and seemingly accepted by Tur and Rambam, is an invalid solution. He derives this interpretation from the fact that the third Baraita of our Gemara deals exclusively with question of Grace after Meals without extrapolating and applying this distinction to prayer. Not only does the third Baraita not draw a distinction between laborers within the case of prayer, but there is also textual evidence that suggests that it supports the opposite approach—all laborers recite the full *Shemoneh Esreh*. This reading is supported by the Baraita's use of the term *"mitpallelin"* when referring to the general act of prayer, which implies that a full *Shemoneh Esreh* should be recited by all laborers.

From the fact that Rif and Rosh only cite the third Baraita, Bach suggests that within the realm of prayer both do not validate any delineation strictly based on the difference between laborers. While Bach admits that there are differences between laborers, there is nothing inherent in these differences that would alter their practice of reciting *Shemoneh Esreh*. However, an external factor might apply differently to the two types of laborers, leading to variance in the law's application to the two groups. Thus, even though Bach writes that a "distinction [between laborers] is ostensibly rejected," he leaves room for the possibility that there is an outside distinction—such as their level of *dechak* (pressure)—that can be applied differently to these respective cases.

Bach continues his commentary by explaining the Gemara's back-and-forth arguments according to his perspective:

ב"ח אורח חיים קי:ד (המשך)

אם כן השתא הא דפריך תלמודא אבריתא דתנא בה הפועלים מתפללין
י"ח והתניא מעין י"ח ואוקמוה באוקימתא בתרא אלא אידי ואידי רבן
גמליאל ולא קשה כאן בעושין בשכרן כאן בעושין בסעודתן ומייתי ראיה
מהך ברייתא דאיכא חילוק בין עושין בשכרן לעושין בסעודתן לענין
ברכת המזון והוא הדין דמחלקינן גבי תפילה דבעושין בשכרן מתפללין
הביננו ובעושין בסעודתן מתפללין י"ח הך אוקימתא ממילא אידחיא דהא
בברייתא גופא קתני סתם קורין קריאת שמע ומתפללין אלמא דאפילו
עושין בשכרן מתפללין י"ח...

Bach, Orach Chaim 110:4 (continued)
If this is so [that there is no inherent difference between laborers], now that which the Talmud asks on the [first] Baraita which says, "Laborers ... recite the [full] eighteen blessings," does not a [second] Baraita say, "A condensed version of the *Shemoneh Esreh*?" and answers by establishing the second distinction: "Rather, both [Baraitot] are the opinion of Rabban Gamliel, and there is no difficulty—[the second statement applies to] wage laborers, and [the first to] those who work only for their meals," and brings proof from that [third] Baraita which distinguishes between wage laborers and those who work only for their meals with regard to the blessing following meals, [deducing that] so too we make this distinction with regard to prayer, that wage laborers recite *Havineinu* and those who work only for their meals recite the [full] eighteen blessings—this distinction is ostensibly rejected, as the [third] Baraita itself simply says "Recite the Shema and pray" [with no further caveats]: apparently, even wage laborers recite [the full] eighteen [blessings]. (Continued below)

Following his conclusion, the second reasoning of the Gemara, that both the Baraitot follow Rabban Gamliel based on a distinction between the laborers, is incorrect. Therefore, in order to resolve the internal contradiction, Bach returns to the first, seemingly rejected approach of the Gemara, which states that the first Baraita follows Rabban Gamliel and the second Rabbi Yehoshua.

ב"ח אורח חיים קי:ד (המשך)

ואם כן ממילא אוקימתא קמא עיקר דקאמר לא קשיא הא רבן גמליאל מתפללין י"ח והא ר' יהושע מתפללין מעין י"ח היינו הביננו...

Bach Orach Chaim 110:4 (continued)

And if this is so, [that the second distinction is invalid,] ostensibly the first distinction is the essential one, the one which said: "This is no difficulty–the statement that the laborers recite the [full] eighteen blessings [reflects the opinion of] Rabban Gamliel, but according Rabbi Yehoshua they recite a condensed version of the *Shemoneh Esreh*, that is, *Havineinu*." (Continued below)

Bach's acceptance of the first approach of the Gemara is not a straightforward solution. As previously mentioned, the Gemara itself finds difficulties with an explanation that ascribes an obvious and limited ruling to Rabbi Yehoshua. Bach suggests a possible resolution to the problem set forth in the Gemara. He also responds to the new difficulty arising from his approach— why, considering the first approach is the accepted resolution, the Gemara would suggest a second.

ב"ח אורח חיים קי:ד (המשך)

ומה שהקשה על זה בגמרא אי ר' יהושע מאי איריא פועלים אפילו כל אדם נמי לאו קושיא היא כלל דכל אדם ודאי רשות הוא להתפלל מעין י"ח לר' יהושע אבל פועלים חובה הוא עליהן להתפלל מעין י"ח שלא לבטל ממלאכת בעל הבית כמו שהקשו התוספות (דף טז עמוד א ד"ה אפילו) אלא דתלמודא הוה קאמר אוקימתא אחריתא כלומר דלדידך נמי דקשיא לך אפילו כל אדם נמי איכא לאוקמי אידי ואידי כרבן גמליאל ולא קשיא כאן בעושין בשכרן כאן בעושין בסעודתן אבל קושטא לאו הכי הוא אלא כאוקימתא קמא הא רבן גמליאל הא ר' יהושע...

Bach, Orach Chaim 110:4 (continued)

And that which the Gemara asked on this, "If so, according to Rabbi Yehoshua, why does the Baraita specify the recitation of a condensed eighteen blessings to laborers? It should be the case for all people!" is no question at all: for all people, it is clearly optional to recite a condensed version of the *Shemoneh Esreh* according to Rabbi Yehoshua, but for laborers it is incumbent upon them to recite the condensed version in order that they not be [exceedingly] idle from the landlord's work (as Tosafot posited in their question). It is just that [in continuing,] the

Talmud was offering another distinction, meaning to say that for
us who presented the difficulty that "it should be the case for all
people," it is also possible to answer that both [Baraitot] are the
opinion of Rabban Gamliel, and there is no difficulty—here [the
second statement applies to] wage laborers, and here [the first]
those who work only for their meals," but, in truth, it is not so;
rather it is as per the first [resolution which makes the]
distinction—this [the first Baraita reflects the opinion of] Rabban
Gamliel and this [the second reflects that of] Rabbi Yehoshua.
(Continued below)

The Gemara raised an objection against attributing the second
Baraita to Rabbi Yehoshua's (who holds that laborers say
Havineinu), stating that this approach offers no novelty. If *all*
people recite *Havineinu*, it would be superfluous to stipulate that
laborers have a similar practice. Bach answers the Gemara's
difficulty by suggesting a possible aspect of novelty in the
formulation that credits the second Baraita to Rabbi Yehoshua.
Rabbi Yehoshua's statement in the Mishnah that all people
should recite *Me'ein Shemoneh Esreh* is a statement of *permission*.
However, in the case of the second Baraita, (whose position is
attributed to Rabbi Yehoshua by the first resolution in the
Gemara), it is "incumbent upon" the laborers to recite *Havineinu*
because they are under various constraints.

So far, based on an understanding of the Gemara gleaned from
Rif and Rosh's versions of the Gemara, Bach has concluded that a
distinction between laborers in regard to prayer is invalid. He
contends that by only citing the third Baraita, Rif and Rosh do not
acknowledge any normative situation where a laborer would
recite *Havineinu*. Thus, Bach rules in accordance with Rabban
Gamliel (who supports the recitation of a full *Shemoneh Esreh*) and
the first approach offered in the Gemara.

ב"ח אורח חיים קי:ד (המשך)

וכיון דהלכתא כרבן גמליאל אף פועלים צריכין להתפלל י"ח בין בעושין
בשכרן בין בעושין בסעודתן דאין להתפלל הבינינו אלא בשעת הדחק כך
הוא מוכרח ממה שכתבו הרי"ף והרא"ש דהכי סבירא להו...

Bach, Orach Chaim 110:4 (continued)

And since the halacha is in accordance with Rabban Gamliel, even laborers must recite the [full] eighteen blessings, whether they are wage laborers or they work only for their meals, as it is only proper to recite *Havineinu* in a case of pressing need (*sha'at ha-dechak*). So must be concluded from the writings of the Rif and Rosh, that this is what they think. (Continued below)

Even though Bach rules in accordance with Rabban Gamliel, he still acknowledges that in *sha'at ha-dechak* one is not obligated to recite *Shemoneh Esreh*. Thus, by explaining Rambam, Tur, Rif, and Rosh with one line of reasoning, Bach has provided a unified approach to the Gemara. However, Rambam's explanation of this Gemara stands in sharp contrast with Bach's interpretation. Rambam's codification follows the distinction set-forth in the second approach of the Gemara, differentiating between wage and food laborers. Bach rejects this distinction and takes an opposite approach. To harmonize and reconcile his new opinion with that of Rambam, Bach explains Rambam as the Tur had explained him.

ב"ח אורח חיים קי:ד (המשך)

ולכן הוה קשיא ליה לרבינו מאי טעמיה דהרמב"ם דפסק כאוקימתא בתרא ודלא כמשמעות הברייתא וקאמר כדי ליישב זה ואפשר שחושב פועלים כשעת הדחק כלומר ועל כן היה מפרש הרמב"ם דגם הברייתא דמחלק בפועלים בברכת המזון בין עושין בשכרן לבין עושין בסעודתן סבירא לה דממילא גם בתפילה בעושין בשכרן צריכין הם למהר למלאכתן ואין להם להתפלל י"ח שלש פעמים ביום דאיכא ביטול מלאכה טובא וחשיב כשעת הדחק אלא יש להם להתפלל הבינינו:

Bach, Orach Chaim 110:4 (continued)

Therefore [because *sha'at ha-dechak* is the sole factor that allows one to recite *Havineinu*], it was a question for our master [Tur], what is the reasoning of the Rambam who ruled according to the second distinction, and not as the [third] Baraita implies? In order to answer this, he said that it is possible that [the Rambam] believes laborers to be a case of pressing need, meaning that consequently the Rambam would explain that the Baraita that distinguishes with regard to the blessings after meals between wage laborers and those who work only for their meals also holds that ostensibly regarding prayer, too, wage laborers need to hurry back to their work and should not recite the [full] eighteen blessings three times daily, as that is a greater form of idling from work and considered to be a case of pressing need (*sha'at ha-dechak*), so instead they should recite *Havineinu*.

According to Tur, Rambam's ruling should not be interpreted as a simple distinction between laborers which seems to "ignore" the third Baraita. Rather, by interpreting the case of laborers working for wages as an instance of *sha'at ha-dechak*, Tur harmonizes Rambam's ruling with the third Baraita.

As previously explained, the third Baraita can be interpreted to rule that there is no legal distinction between laborers. However, there is a practical difference between them, and therefore an outside distinction can be applied to the two groups. As Bach explains "[*Shemoneh Esreh*] is a greater form of idling from work and [wage laborers are] considered to be a case of pressing need (*sha'at ha-dechak*), so instead they should recite *Havineinu*." In this way, Rambam does not base his commentary on a distinction between laborers, but on a valid (previously established) distinction of *sha'at ha-dechak*. In other words, Rambam draws the same distinction as the second reasoning of the Gemara, but on different grounds. The distinguishing factor between the wage earner and the food earner is not theft; rather, it is extenuating circumstance (*sha'at ha-dechak*).

Summary of Bach's interpretation of Berachot 16a:

Underlying approach: Bach accepts the third Baraita as halacha, but does not apply the precedent of making a wage–food distinction to the other Baraitot.

Rationale: The third Baraita referring to a difference between laborers is only dealing with an abridged Grace after Meals, but with regards to prayer, the Baraita rules that a full *Shemoneh Esreh* is appropriate.

Reading of Rosh and Rif: They follow the distinction of the first approach of the Gemara, and rule in accordance with Rabban Gamliel (with the exception of *sha'at ha-dechak*).

Reading of Tur's approach to Rambam: Rambam has the same distinction as second approach in the Gemara, yet not based on inherent distinction between laborers, rather based on applying the distinctions *sha'at ha-dechak* to this case of laborers.

Taz's explanation of Tur — the purpose of Berachot 16a

Taz's commentary on Shulchan Aruch serves as an additional example of an approach that resolves the apparent contradiction between the two Gemarot (Berachot 29a and 16a). In his analysis, Taz takes an approach similar to, yet subtly different from, Bach with regard to *Havineinu*. Like Bach, Taz uses the distinction of *sha'at ha-dechak* to harmonize the conflicting opinions of Rambam and Tur on the one hand and Rif and Rosh on the other. Although utilizing a similar approach, both the starting points and respective conclusions of their arguments differ. Bach's commentary tackles the contradiction between the Gemarot by reinterpreting the case of the laborers and offering a novel reading of the Gemara's structure. Bach's innovative interpretation accommodates both Rif and Rosh's codification of this Gemara and Tur's explanation of Rambam, thus eliminating any contradiction or discrepancy. Taking a different approach, Taz does not address any possible contradiction because he does not think that the texts are dealing with the same issue. In distinction to Bach, Taz starts from the assumption that the Gemara in 29a is the primary discussion of *Havineinu*, and therefore marginalizes the importance of 16a. By downplaying the relevance of this source, essentially contending that the discussions of the two Gemarot are on different planes, Taz eliminates any potential contradiction between the two Gemarot.

Taz outlines what he views to be the primary factor that would allow one to recite *Havineinu*:

ט"ז אורח חיים סימן קי:ב

...אלא נראה דלא כן הוא הדרך דבתפלת השחר הוא עיקר הדין של הבינינו ושם מוכח במסקנא דלא מצלי הבינינו אלא בשעת הדחק מההיא דאביי לייט אמאן דמצלי הבינינו במתא לחד גירסא של התוספות וכמו שכתבו הרי"ף והרא"ש שם...

Taz, Orach Chaim 110:2
[Taz reviews the entire discussion on this Gemara highlighted thus far.] Rather, it seems that [the above] line of understanding

is incorrect. [Instead I suggest,] the fourth chapter of Berachot (entitled *"Tefillat HaShachar"*) contains the central discussion of the law of *Havineinu*. And there it is shown in the Talmud's conclusion that one only recites *Havineinu* in a case of extenuating circumstances (*sha'at ha-dechak*) from the fact that "Abaye placed a curse upon those who recite '*Havineinu*' in the city," according to one textual variant of Tosafot and as the Rif and the Rosh wrote in their commentaries there." (Continued below)

Taz strengthens his assertion, stating that the Gemara discussing the laborers follows the same distinction:

ט"ז אורח חיים סימן קי:ב (המשך)

במסקנת התלמוד דנחתינן לזה להכריע בין דחק או לא ותו אין חילוק אחר
הכי קיימא לן וכן כתבו הפוסקים לחלק כן ונמצא שמה שכתב הרמב"ם
לחלק בין עושין בשכרן או לא וכבר חילק הוא עצמו בין דחק או לא קשה
עליו כיון שיש שיש חילוק בין דחק או לא תו ליכא חילוק אחר דהני הכרעות
התלמוד לחלק דוקא בין שעת הדחק...

Taz, Orach Chaim 110:2 (continued)
The Talmud's ultimate conclusion is that we do, indeed, accept the distinction of pressing circumstances to the exclusion of all others—and this is the way the halacha is established. And the decisors (Rif and Rosh) also wrote this as the sole distinction. Consequently, that which the Rambam wrote to distinguish between wage laborers and non-[wage laborers, i.e., those paid in food] after he, himself, had already distinguished between pressure situations and not becomes rather difficult, for now that the Talmud distinguishes between pressure situations and all others, there should be no further distinction—for that was the particular distinction that the Talmud brought between *sha'at ha-dechak* [and otherwise]... (Continued below)

As the basis of his discussion, Taz contends that the Gemara in 29a "contains the central discussion of the law of *Havineinu*." Like Bach, Taz strictly maintains that the distinction drawn by Berachot 29a—*sha'at ha-dechak* is the sole mitigating factor that would allow one to recite *Havineinu*. Taz clearly states, "now that the Talmud distinguishes between pressure situations and all others there should be no further distinction." Thus it follows that this factor exists to the "exclusion of all other" factors (including a distinction between laborers based on theft). Taz explains Rambam's commentary in this perspective:

ט"ז אורח חיים סימן קי:ב (המשך)

ועל זה כתב רבינו הטור ואפשר שחושב פועלים כשעת הדחק דהיינו חילוק זה דעושין בשכרן הוה ליה כשעת הדחק אבל בשכר סעודתן הוה ליה שלא כשעת הדחק ונמצא שפיר כתב רבינו הטור דין זה בשם הרמב"ם דוקא כן נראה לי נכון בס"ד:

Taz, Orach Chaim 110:2 (continued)

For this reason [i.e., *sha'at ha-dechak* is the sole mitigating factor], our master the Tur wrote "it is possible that he [Rambam] believes laborers to be a case of pressing circumstances." That is, the distinction is that those who work for wages are equivalent to a case of pressing circumstances, but those who work solely for food are not in pressing circumstances. It thus appears that our master the Tur was indeed correct in indicating that this ruling is specifically in the name of the Rambam. Such appears to me to be correct with the aid of heaven.

In his commentary Taz shares Bach's insistence on the correctness of Tur's reading of Rambam. Both acknowledge that Rambam's distinction in the case of the laborers is drawn strictly on the factor of *sha'at ha-dechak*. Although the ruling in this case resembles that in the Gemara in Berachot 16a, the motivations differ. Therefore, Tur was correct in attributing Rambam's ruling to logic that was outside of this Gemara.

Tur has identified what he considers to be the main factor influencing the recitation of *Havineinu*, and he has shown how Rambam could be interpreted to follow this reasoning. However, by placing the primary importance on the Gemara in 29a, the relevance of the Gemara in 16a is put into question. Although similar in many respects, Taz's interpretation of the purpose of the Gemara in Berachot 16a diverges significantly from Bach. While Berachot 16a's purpose does not lie in advancing the concept of *Havineinu*, it does serve in clarifying the technical issue of with which Tanna the halacha accords. Because Taz views the function of Berachot 16a to be different from the function of Berachot 29a, he has no logical impetus to resolve the conflict between the two Gemarot; in his view there is none.

ט"ז אורח חיים סימן קי:ב (המשך)

ואם כן צריך לומר דפסק התלמוד התם דלא כחד דלרבן גמליאל צריך
לעולם י"ח ולרבי יהושע לעולם הביננו והתלמוד מכריע להלכה דבשעת
הדחק יש לסמוך על ר' יהושע ושלא בשעת הדחק עבדינן כר' גמליאל
ובפרק היה קורא מפלפל בגמרא כמאן מן התנאים אתיא ההיא ברייתא
דיאמרו הבינינו דשם לא נחתי כלל לחלק בין דחק או לא אלא בדברי
התנאים עצמן מפלפל שם כמאן אתיא ועל זה פרכינן אי ר' יהושע מאי
אריא פועלים ולא סלקינן שם להאי סברא דיש חילוק בין דחק או לא.

Taz, Orach Chaim 110:2 (continued)

If so, we must say that the Talmud did not rule in accordance
with any of the Tannaitic opinions, for according to Rabban
Gamliel one must always say *Shemoneh Esreh,* and according to
Rabbi Yehoshua one always says *Havineinu,* but the Talmud
ultimately concluded as a matter of halacha that in a time of
pressing need (*sha'at ha-dechak*) one may rely on Rabbi Yehoshua,
but otherwise the practice is in accordance with Rabban Gamliel.
*The back-and-forth in the second chapter of Berachot (16a) simply seeks
to harmonize the conflicting Baraitot[7] with the views of the Tannaim
(Rabban Gamliel and Rabbi Yehoshua) who say that laborers recite
Havineinu—there the Gemara does not at all suppose a distinction
between pressing need and not. Rather, it conjectures about whose
opinion the two Baraitot follow.* [Emphasis added.] It then rejects
this approach by asking, if the second Baraita is the opinion of
Rabbi Yehoshua, why is it limited to laborers; it should be the
case for everyone? But the Gemara there does not conclude with
the   rationale   which   differentiates   between   pressing
circumstances and not.

According to Taz's approach, the halacha combines multiple
opinions expressed in the Gemara and follows the position of
Abaye. Ideally one should follow the practice of Rabban Gamliel,
but in times of pressing need, *sha'at ha-dechak,* it is permissible to
rely on Rabbi Yehoshua's lenient practice.

Summary of Berachot 16a according to Taz:

Underlying approach: Berachot 16a is only trying to
determine to whom in the Mishnah to ascribe the halacha. The
primary discussion about the nature of *Havineinu* is on

---

[7] Taz's language refers particularly to the second Baraita which raises the
issue of *Havineinu.*

Berachot 29a, where it is established that the main factor that allows an individual to recite *Havineinu* is *sha'at ha-dechak*.

Reading of Rosh and Rif: They consider the third Baraita as the halacha, yet they do not subscribe to any of the other content of this section of the Gemara.

Reading of Tur's approach to Rambam: Even though it appears like the Rambam accepts the second approach of the Gemara, this is not the case; he is just applying the distinction of *sha'at ha-dechak* to the scenario of the Gemara.

Peri Chadash's approach — Abaye's opinion

Peri Chadash takes a similar viewpoint to Taz and Bach, rejecting the distinction between laborers. The primary difference between the commentators in this area is in regard to their formulation. Whereas Taz sees the halacha to be a type of compromise between Rabban Gamliel and Rabbi Yehoshua following the stipulation of Abaye, the Peri Chadash views the halacha to be completely in accordance with Abaye.

פרי חדש או"ח קי ס"ק ב

ולכן נראה לי דסבירא ליה להטור ז"ל דאע"ג דבהני ברייתות קתני שפועלים העושין בשכרן מתפללים מעין י"ח לא קיימא לן הכי (מוכח) [מכוח] ההיא דאביי לייט אמאן דמצלי הבינינו [ברכות כט, א] אם לא בשעת הדחק, והאמורא יש כח לו לפסוק הפך הברייתא, וכיון דכן, לדידן דקיימא לן כאביי דדוקא בשעת הדחק יתפלל הבינינו, בפועלים דליכא שעת הדחק יראה ודאי שצריכין להתפלל י"ח, ולכן כתב הטור שאין ישוב לדברי הרמב"ם ז"ל אם לא שחושב פועלים בשעת הדחק כן נראה לי.

Peri Chadash, Orach Chaim 110:2

Therefore, it seems to me that the Tur, of blessed memory, was of the opinion that even though in those Baraitot (Berachot 16a) it says that wage laborers recite a condensed version of *Shemoneh Esreh*, we do not rule accordingly from the force of the Talmudic passage (Berachot 29a) in which Abaye placed a curse upon those who recite *Havineinu*, unless it is a case of pressing circumstances—an Amora does have the ability to rule contrary to a Baraita [just not a Mishnah]. As such, for us, who rule in accordance with Abaye that only in pressing circumstances may one say *Havineinu*, with laborers, where no pressing circumstances exist, it would seem that they certainly must recite [the full] *Shemoneh Esreh*. Therefore, the Tur wrote that there is no explanation for the Rambam's ruling unless he believes that laborers are a case of pressing circumstances—so it seems to me.

Instead of formulating the resolution as a compromise between two positions, Peri Chadash attributes the halacha to one opinion—that of Abaye. Abaye's status as an Amora allows him to overturn the Baraita that would permit laborers to recite *Havineinu*. Abaye limits the recitation of *Havineinu* strictly to circumstances of *sha'at ha-dechak*, and this is the final halacha according to Peri Chadash. (See Table 2.1.)

While approaching the text with different viewpoints and interpretations, Bach, Taz and Peri Chadash arrive at the same conclusion—*sha'at ha-dechak* is the only factor that would influence the recitation of *Havineinu*. Mindful of this stipulation, they state that the halacha follows Rabban Gamliel. (Note: although similar in practice to this ruling, Peri Chadash rules exclusively in accordance with Abaye.) Their observations and opinions on this law reflect an incorporation of various seemingly conflicting sources, which they harmonize in a unified approach. By not settling for a superficial understanding of the Gemara that would gloss over contradictions and subtleties within the text, the commentators establish a more complete construct of *Havineinu* as presented in Berachot 16a, as well as recast the understanding of *Havineinu* in Berachot 29a.

At this point, the relationship between the two Gemarot is apparent. The sole factor that would allow one to recite *Havineinu*—*sha'at ha-dechak*—established in Berachot 29a is also, according to this reading of Rambam, the sole factor in Berachot 16a. As evidenced by the relative emphasis placed on the reading of the two principal Gemarot in question (16a and 29a), it can be seen that the Gemara in 29a "contains the central discussion of the law of *Havineinu*." It is in this Gemara that the "Talmud's conclusion that one only recites *Havineinu* in a case of emergent need (*sha'at ha-dechak*)" emerges. These commentators view *sha'at ha-dechak* as the underlying concept behind all the commentaries— Rambam and Tur as well as Rif and Rosh.

Table 2.1
Berachot 16a according to Taz and Bach

Resolution of contradictory Baraitot	Commentary	Difficulty	Solution	Textual proof
First answer of the Gemara: Rabban Gamliel vs. Rabbi Yehoshua	Bach	Why are laborers singled out for Rabbi Yehoshua – no novelty in this position?	Everyone has option to say *Havineinu*, but laborers have an obligation to do so	Solution put-forth by Tosafot
	Taz	Taz follows the simple reading of the text, which rejects the first reasoning of the Gemara	Dispute is about whom to attribute the halacha, not in which situations *Havineinu* permitted	
Second answer of the Gemara: Wage earner vs. Food earner	Bach	Third Baraita says simply "*mitpallelin*," meaning recite *Shemoneh Esreh*; therefore, third Baraita cannot be used as precedent for distinction between wage–food laborers	Reject distinction between wage and food earners; second resolution is quoted as Rambam and interpreted by the Tur within the context of *dechak*	Rif and Rosh quote third Baraita only regarding Grace after Meals, without deriving any laws of prayer
	Taz	How can we draw this distinction at all – sole distinguishing factor is that of *sha'at ha-dechak*?	Dispute is about whom to attribute the halacha, not in which situations *Havineinu* permitted	Rabban Gamliel making exception based on theft; from Berachot 29 (Abaye's curse) only exceptions are cases of *dechak* – this opinion in line with Abaye

Just as Berachot 29a's interpretation influenced the interpretation of Berachot 16a, Berachot 16a has expanded the definition established in Berachot 29a. Whereas previously *sha'at ha-dechak* included traveling and times of compromised *kavvanah*, now Rambam and Tur have expanded the term to incorporate a situation of the hurried worker, pressed for time.

2.2 Reassessing Rambam—incorporating the view of Rabbi Akiva

In describing who may and may not recite *Havineinu*, Rambam differentiates between paid laborers and those who work merely for their meals. This codification of the laws of *Havineinu* has been subject to much interpretation. Tur proposes that Rambam's distinguishing criterion for this prayer is actually *sha'at ha-dechak*. Bach, Taz, and Peri Chadash all see Rambam's codification in Mishneh Torah as representing the opinions of Rabban Gamliel, Rabbi Yehoshua, or Abaye. However, when looking into a broader range of Rambam's sources it becomes evident that there are many other possible factors he may consider. This section explores the possibility that Rambam's ruling follows the position of Rabbi Akiva in the Mishnah, cited below:

משנה מסכת ברכות פרק ד משנה ג

רבן גמליאל אומר בכל יום מתפלל אדם שמונה עשרה רבי יהושע אומר מעין שמונה עשרה ר' עקיבא אומר אם שגורה תפלתו בפיו יתפלל שמונה עשרה ואם לאו מעין י"ח

Mishnah, Berachot 4:3
Rabban Gamliel says: every day a person recites eighteen blessings (*Shemoneh Esreh*). Rabbi Yehoshua says: a condensed version of the eighteen blessings (*Me'ein Shemoneh Esreh*); Rabbi Akiva says: if prayer is very familiar to him (literally, dwells upon his lips), he should recite eighteen blessings; if not, a condensed version of the eighteen (*Me'ein Shemoneh Esreh*).

Although presenting distinct positions concerning the recitation of *Havineinu*, these opinions in the Mishnah can all be interpreted to accord with Rambam's reading of the Gemara as related in his work Mishneh Torah. Viewed in line with Rabban Gamliel's statement, perhaps Rambam sees *Shemoneh Esreh* as the ideal option for everyday prayer, only to be changed in a case of *sha'at ha-dechak* (as per the Tur). Thus, "every day a person recites eighteen blessings (*Shemoneh Esreh*)," except in extreme extenuating circumstances. Alternatively, Rambam, while still considering *Shemoneh Esreh* as the optimum prayer, could rule in accordance with Rabbi Yehoshua. According to this interpretation, "a condensed version of the eighteen blessings (*Me'ein Shemoneh Esreh*)" is a general path of action that may be followed daily, under any circumstances. However, laborers who are paid actual wages have no option of reciting the *Shemoneh Esreh* (as suggested by Bach) due to concern of theft from the employer. Therefore, it is mandatory to recite *Havineinu* in this case. When trying to match Rambam's position concerning *Havineinu* and the mitigating factor of *sha'at ha-dechak* with Rabbi Akiva, a potential difficulty arises. Rambam's position has different parameters than Rabbi Akiva's statement; Rambam only allows the recitation of *Havineinu* by wage-laborers, while Rabbi Akiva allows anyone who lacks proficiency to recite it. Even if one were to accept Tur's reading of Rambam, Rambam would only allow *Havineinu* to be recited during *sha'at ha-dechak*. The next source will show that Rambam permits the recitation of *Havineinu* in much broader circumstances. This points toward a reading of Rambam that is in line with Rabbi Akiva.

In his commentary on the Mishnah, Rambam explicitly rules in accordance with Rabbi Akiva:

רמב"ם פרוש המשניות ברכות ד:ג

הלכה כרבי עקיבא. ופירוש שגורה שלא נתבלבל לשונו אבל אומר במהירות ורגילות.

Rambam, Commentary on the Mishnah, Berachot 4:3
The law follows Rabbi Akiva. The meaning of the phrase "familiar to him (literally, dwells on his lips – *shegurah*)" is one whose speech does not get confused; rather, he says [the prayers] with speed and regularity.

Here, Rambam explains Rabbi Akiva's phrase "to dwell on one's lips" denotes familiarity with the prayer to the extent that one does not stumble on the words and is able to pray efficiently and confidently. Rambam does not make any mention of "*sha'at ha-dechak*" as a circumstance in which *Havineinu* can be recited. However, in the Hilchot Tefillah (Laws of Prayer) section of

Mishneh Torah, Rambam broadens his formulation of times when it is appropriate to recite *Havineinu* to include both *sha'at ha-dechak* as well as unfamiliarity with prayer.

רמב"ם הלכות תפילה ונשיאת כפים פרק ב הלכה ב

בכל תפלה שבכל יום מתפלל אדם תשע עשרה ברכות אלו על הסדר, במה דברים אמורים כשמצא דעתו מכוונת ולשונו תמהר לקרות אבל אם היה טרוד ודחוק או שקצרה לשונו מהתפלל יתפלל שלש ראשונות וברכה אחת מעין כל האמצעיות ושלש אחרונות ויצא ידי חובתו.

Rambam, Mishneh Torah, Hilchot Tefillah 2:2

In every prayer of every day, one should recite these nineteen blessings (*Shemoneh Esreh*) in order. When does this apply? When one has proper intent (*kavvanah*; literally, one's mind is directed), and is able to pray nimbly (literally, one's tongue can recite quickly). However, if one is preoccupied (*tarud*) or pressed (*dechak*), or if one has difficulty composing one's prayers (literally, one's tongue is short of prayer), one should recite the first three [blessings], a single blessing that is an abstraction of all the middle ones, and the last three [blessings], and one has [thereby] fulfilled one's obligation.

Among the factors that would permit one to recite *Havineinu* Rambam lists: one who lacks *kavvanah*, is unable to pray nimbly, is preoccupied, is pressed, and has difficulty composing one's prayers.

Accordingly, Rav Ovadiah of Bartenura (15th century, Italy) in his own commentary on the Mishnah attributes the halacha to Rabbi Akiva:

ר' עובדיה מברטנורה, ברכות פרק ד משנה ג, ד"ה שגורה בפיו

שהוא למוד ורגיל בה. והלכה כר' עקיבא שמי שאין תפילתו שגורה בפיו או בשעת הדחק מתפלל אדם שלש ראשונות ושלש אחרונות והבינינו באמצע שהיא מעין כל האמצעיות.

R. Ovadiah Bartenura, Mishnah Berachot 4:3, s.v. *shegurah be-fiv*

That he is learned and accustomed to [saying] it. And the law follows Rabbi Akiva, that one whose prayer does not dwell on his lips or is in a time of pressure (*sha'at ha-dechak*) should recite the first three blessings, the last three blessings, and in between *Havineinu*—which is an abstraction of the middle [blessings].

This source is additional evidence of a firmly established tradition among medieval commentators to accept Rabbi Akiva's position. Here, as in Rambam's commentary, both proficiency and *sha'at ha-dechak* are factors in *Havineinu*, showing a strong connection between Rabbi Akiva's position of fluency and the general ruling of *sha'at ha-dechak*.

Aruch HaShulchan clarifies Rambam's opinion in the Mishnah:

ערוך השלחן אורח חיים קי:ב

...ולדבריו מה שאמר ר' עקיבא אם שגורה וכו' ואם לאו יתפלל מעין י"ח הך לאו הכי פרושו או שאינה שגורה בפיו מחמת קצירת לשונו או מחמת טירדה ודחקות:

Aruch HaShulchan, Orach Chaim 110:2
According to [Rambam], that which Rabbi Akiva said, "If it is familiar...and if not, [he should recite] an abstraction of *Shemoneh Esreh*," is not to be taken narrowly; rather, it means to say either it is not familiar to him due to a shortness in his speech or due to trouble (*tirdah*) or pressure (*dechak*).

Commenting on Rambam's opinion of Rabbi Akiva's position, Aruch HaShulchan quotes both reasons why one would say an abridged version: due to "shortness of speech" and "troubles or pressure." Aruch HaShulchan basically views *dechak* (pressure) and *tarud* (trouble) as thematic extensions of the example provided by Rabbi Akiva in the Mishnah. Coming to explain various reasons to recite *Havineinu*, Aruch HaShulchan, like Rambam, not only cites *dechak* but *tarud* as well.

Meiri's commentary identifies the logical connection between proficiency and *sha'at ha-dechak*. Meiri associates Rabbi Akiva's approach not only with the principle of technical proficiency but also that of *kavvanah*. This becomes a key distinction between Rabbi Akiva and Rabbi Yehoshua.

המאירי בית הבחירה ברכות כח עמוד ב–ל עמוד א

המשנה השלישית ... ופירוש שגורה שלא יתבלבל לשונו אבל אומר אותה במהירות ורגילות והלכה כר' עקיבא.

אמר המאירי רבן גמליאל אומר בכל יום ויום מתפלל אדם י"ח ואינו רשאי לפטור עצמו בברכה מעין י"ח והיא כוללת כל האמצעיות ר' יהושע

אומר שיכול הוא אם הוא טרוד לפטור עצמו בכל יום ויום במעין י"ח
רצונו לומר ג' ראשונות וג' אחרונות וברכה אמצעית שכוללת כל
האמצעיות אף על פי שאנשי כנסת הגדולה י"ח תקנו ושהוא יכול לכוין
דעתו לכלם מכל מקום הואיל ודרך כלל כלל כלהו איתנהו בה והוא יש לו איזו
טרדא אף על פי שהוא יכול לכוין לכלם יכול לפטור עצמו בה ר' עקיבא
אומר אם שגורה תפלתו בפיו רצונו לומר שבקי בשמנה עשרה ויכול
לכוין בהם יתפלל י"ח ואין טרדתו מעכבתו ואם לאו לא יתפלל מעין י"ח
מוטב שיקצר ויכוין משיאריך ולא יכוין.

Meiri, Beit HaBechirah Commentary to Berachot 28b–30a

The third Mishnah … and the meaning of "dwells" is that one's tongue not become confused, rather one says it quickly and regularly. And the halacha follows Rabbi Akiva.

Said the Meiri – Rabban Gamliel says: Each and every day one recites eighteen blessings, and one is not permitted to acquit oneself by saying a blessing that is a condensed version of the *Shemoneh Esreh*, which includes all the middle [blessings].

Rabbi Yehoshua says that one can, if one is encumbered, acquit oneself every day with a condensed version of *Shemoneh Esreh*, meaning to say the first three [blessings] and the last three [blessings], and a middle blessing that includes all the middle [blessings of *Shemoneh Esreh*]. Even though the Men of the Great Assembly instituted eighteen [full blessings], and even if one would be able to have full intent (*kavvanah*) for all of them— nevertheless, since, generally speaking, all [of the blessings] are included in it (*Havineinu*), and one is indeed (even minimally) encumbered, even though one is able to concentrate (*lekhavvein*) for all [of the blessings], one can acquit oneself with [a condensed version of *Shemoneh Esreh*].

Rabbi Akiva says, "If the prayer dwells upon his lips," meaning to say that if one is an expert (fluent) in [the full] *Shemoneh Esreh*, and is able to have proper concentration (*lekhavven*) for [the blessings], one should recite [a full] eighteen [blessings] (*Shemoneh Esreh*), and one's encumbrance does not prevent him [from being able to concentrate]. If [one is] not [comfortable with the text], one should recite a condensed version of *Shemoneh Esreh*—it is better for one to shorten and concentrate than to lengthen and not concentrate.

According to Meiri, Rabban Gamliel not only views the full *Shemoneh Esreh* as a preferable prayer, but as an obligatory one, and no other version of these eighteen blessings will suffice in any circumstance. Rabbi Yehoshua, in contrast, allows one to recite an abridged version in a time of burden (*tarud*). This opinion reflects the fundamental belief that *Havineinu* is sufficient for fulfilling the minimum obligation of prayer. Significantly, Rabbi Yehoshua does not see the additional concern of the ability to concentrate to be a factor in this formulation.

Rabbi Akiva's position differs from Rabbi Yehoshua's regarding the issue of *kavvanah*. To Rabbi Akiva, it is the element of *kavvanah* that is the determining factor that influences the recitation of *Havineinu*. If one is able to have *kavvanah*, one should say a full *Shemoneh Esreh*; otherwise, a condensed version is optimal. Meiri explains the reasoning behind this position: it is better to say less (i.e., *Havineinu*) and have *kavvanah* than to say more (i.e., the full *Shemoneh Esreh*) and not have *kavvanah*.

Meiri's approach to the Mishnah is different than the one presented earlier in this chapter. Above, each position was evaluated and interpreted in accordance with Rambam's opinion. Meiri's presentation of the Mishnah differs in that he reads Rabban Gamliel's and Rabbi Yehoshua's positions as standing on their own, and does not attempt to integrate their positions with Rambam's. The two interpretations of the Mishnah are outlined in Table 2.2.

Meiri clearly outlines the connection between fluency and concentration. Lack of proficiency, explains Meiri, hampers a person's ability to concentrate on the meaning behind the words. He presents the concept of lack of concentration as the underlying concept behind Rabbi Akiva's formulation. Whereas *dechak* is a type of external situational pressure, *kavvanah* is an internal one.

Meiri's commentary culminates with the ruling that the halacha is in accordance with Rabbi Akiva:

המאירי בית הבחירה ברכות כח עמוד ב–ל עמוד א (המשך)

זהו ביאור המשנה והלכה כר' עקיבא שכל הבקי מתפלל בכל יום י"ח ועוד אחרת עמהם שהוסיפו בה ביבנה והיא ברכת המינים וצריך שיאמרם על הסדר שנסדרו ואם היה בדרך או שעת הטירדה עד שלא מצא דעתו מכוונת מתפלל ג' ראשונות וג' אחרונות וברכה מעין אמצעיות באמצע.

Table 2.2
Two interpretations of Mishnah Berachot 4:3

	Rabban Gamliel	Rabbi Yehoshua	Rabbi Akiva	Conclusion about Rambam's position
Each interpreted in line with Rambam	Views *Havineinu* as the optimal prayer for a case of *dechak*	Permits *Havineinu* to be recited by everyone in all circumstances. Wage laborers are obligated to recite *Havineinu*	He has a wider exception to the general rule of Rabban Gamliel, in that he allows it in *dechak* and in lack of fluency situations	Because Rambam's formulation includes elements of *dechak, tirdah, kavvanah,* and fluency, Rabbi Akiva's maximally inclusive position is what Rambam considers to be accurate
Meiri's interpretation	Categorically denies any possibility of reciting *Havineinu*	Allows for *Havineinu* very freely (in any situation of encumbrance), even when one is able to concentrate, because Rabbi Yehoshua fundamentally believes it fulfills the minimum requirement	Only allows in scenarios of lacking *kavvanah*	Because Rambam provides specific criteria for the recitation of *Havineinu,* it cannot be that he holds like either Rabban Gamliel (who always prohibits the recitation of *Havineinu*) or Rabbi Yehoshua (who always allows it)

Meiri, Beit HaBechirah Commentary to Berachot 28b–30a (continued)

This is the explanation of the Mishnah, and the *halacha* follows Rabbi Akiva, that everyone who is expert (fluent) recites [full] eighteen blessings (*Shemoneh Esreh*) every day, along with another [blessing] that was added in Yavneh (the nineteenth blessing added to *Shemoneh Esreh*), which is the blessing regarding the heretics, and one must say them in the order that they were set. But if one was traveling (literally, on the road) or [in] a time of encumbrance, so much so that one finds one's mind unable to concentrate (*mekhuvvenet*), one recites the first three [blessings] and the last three [blessings], and a blessing that is an abstraction of the middle [blessings] in the middle. [The commentary proceeds to quote the text of *Havineinu*.]

Understanding Meiri's reading in connection to the Laborers

Meiri's commentary clearly establishes the logical link between Rabbi Akiva's approach, as supported by Rambam, and the situation with the laborers in Berachot 16a. Why does the Gemara not mention Rabbi Akiva's position? Additionally, why would Bach and Taz rule that the halacha is in accordance to Rabban Gamliel?

According to Meiri, because the Gemara makes exceptions in which one is allowed to recite *Havineinu*, the ultimate ruling of the Gemara follows Rabbi Akiva's position. Rabban Gamliel's position, "every day a person recites eighteen blessings," is not flexible and does not allow for situations where one could recite *Havineinu*, whereas Rabbi Akiva's position does. Thus, Rabban Gamliel's position as presented in the Gemara does not reflect his true opinion (as expressed in the Mishnah). Rather, it represents his opinion in light of the general acceptance of Rabbi Akiva's position. Ideally, Rabban Gamliel rules that *Havineinu* should not be said. However, once the Gemara concedes that there are circumstances where *Havineinu* is permitted, Rabban Gamliel communicates which situations would, in his opinion, be appropriate to allow *Havineinu*. Since the ruling follows Rabbi Akiva, Rabban Gamliel accepts a leniency in a situation of potential theft. Essentially, Rabban Gamliel defers to Rabbi Akiva's position. In this way, Rambam is able to rule in accordance with Rabbi Akiva in Berachot 16a while simultaneously accepting Rabban Gamliel's leniency based on theft.

Meiri clearly states the position in the Mishnah with which the law is in accordance. Additionally, Rabban Gamliel's position in the Gemara has been explained so that Meiri's interpretation is still valid. Taking these two perspectives into account, what is Meiri's ultimate reading of the Gemara? Meiri, like Rambam, rules according to Rabbi Akiva, per the second approach within the Gemara which attributed both cases to Rabban Gamliel with the distinction of wage versus food earners regarding prayer.

המאירי בית הבחירה ברכות טז עמוד א

האומנין שהן נשכרין אצל בעל הבית ויש הפסד לבה"ב בביטולן קורין בראש האילן אם מלאכתם שם כדי לפסגו או לאיזה ענין או בראש הנדבך כלומר טורי האבנים שבכותל שהוא בונה ואעפ"י שאין הכונה מצויה כל כך במקומות אלו מכל מקום אנו חוששין להפסדו של בעל הבית...מה שאין רשאין לעשות כן בתפילה שהתפילה צריך בה כונה יתרה וצריכין לירד מן האילן או מן הכותל...

פועלים שהיו עושין מלאכה אצל בעל הבית אם היו עושין בשכרן קורין ק"ש בברכותיה ומתפללין ג' ראשונות וג' אחרונות וברכת הביננו באמצע שהיא כוללת כל האמצעיות...ואם לא היו נוטלין שכר אלא שהיו עושין בסעודתן קורין ק"ש בברכותיה ומתפללין י"ח ואוכלין פתן ומברכין לפניה המוציא ואחריה ד' ברכות כתקנן.

Meiri, Beit HaBechirah Commentary to Berachot 16a

If laborers working for the employer will cause a loss to the employer with their wasting of time (by climbing down the tree or wall in order to say Shema, then climbing back up), they should say Shema at the top of the tree if they are working there in order to prune it or for some other matter, or at the top of a wall, meaning courses of stones atop the wall that he is building—even though it is somewhat difficult to have appropriate intent (kavvanah) in such places, nonetheless we are concerned for the landlord's loss... However, [laborers] are not permitted to do so for [the Shemoneh Esreh], as it requires greater intent—they must descend from the tree or from the wall.

Laborers that are doing work for an employer, if they are wage laborers, they say Shema with its blessings, and they recite the first three and last three blessings and the Havineinu blessing in the middle which includes all the middle [blessings]...And if they were not receiving wages, rather they were working for their meals, they say Shema with its blessings, they recite full Shemoneh Esreh, and they eat their bread and make the blessing [on the bread] before [they eat], and the four blessings [to be recited] after [they eat] as they were instituted.

Like Rambam, Meiri accepts the second resolution in the Gemara and its clear grounding of the permission to recite *Havineinu* on theft on the part of the laborer, as Meiri says that taking the time to recite the full *Shemoneh Esreh* "will cause a loss to the employer."

Notably, *kavvanah* is the unifying consideration of both types of laborers, despite the difference of ruling in each case. With regard to the sustenance laborer, who is permitted to use more time for personal matters (because there is no concern for the landlords loss), he is required to recite a full *Shemoneh Esreh*. In order to do so, Meiri stipulates, he must climb down from the tree because the *Shemoneh Esreh* "requires greater intent." Although the wage laborer is not allowed as much freedom in using the employer's time for personal use, he too has to take *kavvanah* into consideration when praying. Therefore, to ensure the proper intent during prayer, he recites *Havineinu*. While under different obligations to the employer, both types of laborers are under the same obligations for prayer—to have proper intent—and appropriate measures must be taken to insure this is met.

Meiri's commentary stands in stark contrast to the explanations of Bach and Taz. While all are coming to understand the Gemara, they do so following different paths. Bach and Taz re-examine the Gemara, critically analyzing it in an attempt to follow the established principle of *sha'at ha-dechak* and ruled that the halacha is in accordance with Rabban Gamliel. Meiri, following Rabbi Akiva, seeks to explain how his reading of the Gemara is a natural outgrowth of Rabbi Akiva's position.

In addition to these perspectives which rule in accordance with either Rabban Gamliel or Rabbi Akiva, there is a third line of thought—one which attributes the halacha to Rabbi Yehoshua's opinion. In Eshkol's formulation of the halacha, he cites the text of *Havineinu* in Rabbi Yehoshua's name:

ספר האשכול (אלבק) לקוטי הלכות תפילה דף לג עמוד ב
ר' יהושע אומר מעין י"ח, והיינו הבינונו...

Sefer HaEshkol (Albeck ed.), Laws of Prayer 33b
Rabbi Yehoshua says, a condensed version of *Shemoneh Esreh*
which is: "Grant us (*Havineinu*)..." [The commentary continues
with the text of *Havineinu*.]

Although Eshkol does not provide the reasoning for his ruling,
there are several conceivable possibilities. One, very similar to
Bach and Taz's reading, is that Rabbi Yehoshua's view—*Me'ein
Shemoneh Esreh*—is not intended as the everyday ruling, but rather
(in conjunction with Rabban Gamliel, and following Abaye's
stipulation) a prayer intended for certain circumstances.

Despite the difference in methods, all these commentaries reach
amazingly uniform rulings. This similarity will be explored
further in the next section.

A broad evaluation; a uniform result

The concept of *dechak* was not invented by Rabbeinu Channanel
or Rif. Rather, it seems that it was conceded by all three of the
Tannaim (sages) in the Mishnah. Even Rabbi Yehoshua would
agree that the ideal is the format established by the pre-Mishnah
sages. As Meiri comments, "Rabbi Yehoshua says that one may
[say *Havineinu*...]—even though the Men of the Great Assembly
(*Anshei Kenesset HaGedolah*) instituted that we should recite
eighteen blessings." By the same token, even Rabban Gamliel
makes an exception, allowing *Havineinu* in the case of the laborers,
as explained by Bach and Taz. Additionally, according to the
reading of Bach and Taz, who follow Abaye, the Gemara in 29a is
a combination of the two Tannaim (sages of the Mishnah). The
Taz writes, "But the Talmud ultimately concluded that in a time
of pressing need (*sha'at ha-dechak*) one may rely on Rabbi Yehoshua,
but otherwise the practice is in accordance with Rabban Gamliel."
As clearly outlined in the proceeding section, Rabbi Akiva's
position is represented in the Gemara as well. The disagreement
between the Tannaim is not about the concept of *dechak*, but about
the *degree* of *dechak*. While some limit *dechak* to situations of
traveling, others, like Meiri, include *kavvanah*, proficiency, and
precautions against theft in the category of *dechak* as well.

We thus see that various commentators offer differing approaches to the Mishnah. Yet, each of the positions represented in the Mishnah, when interpreted along a specific line of reasoning, can be seen as reaching the same conclusion. (See Table 2.3.)

Notably, none of the opinions cited absolutely forbids the recitation of *Havineinu*. From this it would seem that the contemporary practice ought to reflect this attitude—although not always to be recited, *Havineinu* is a legitimate prayer that can be recited in times of need. The modern day practice will be discussed at length in Chapter Four. Before that, Chapter Three will address the times throughout the year when one might not be able to recite the *Havineinu* prayer. In this section, more so than what we have seen to this point, the multiplicity of opinions *within* the Gemara will lead to the differing rulings within the halacha.

Table 2.3
Summary of conclusions

Opinion in Mishnah	Modification	Comments	Who asserts this view	Conclusion
Rabban Gamliel	Rely on Rabbi Yehoshua in times of *dechak*	Exception for laborers working is *dechak*, according to Rambam	Tur, Bach, and Taz's presentation of Rambam	*Havineinu* is allowed in a time of *dechak*
Rabbi Yehoshua	When seen in conjunction with Rabban Gamliel, and only follows in times of *dechak*	Exception for laborers working is *dechak*, according to Rambam	Eshkol	*Havineinu* is allowed in a time of *dechak*
Rabbi Akiva	Lack of proficiency interpreted to include *kavvanah*; no possibility of *kavvanah* is called *tarud*, which is likened to *dechak*	Opinion not even cited in Tur	Rambam, Meiri	*Havineinu* is allowed in a time of *dechak*

Chapter Three
Limits on reciting *Havineinu*
Avoiding encumbrance and misconceptions

The previous chapters outlined situations in which one is permitted to recite *Havineinu* instead of the full *Shemoneh Esreh*: pressing circumstances, collectively categorized as *sha'at ha-dechak*. However, there are times when *Havineinu* theoretically could be permitted but is unworkable practically, because of modifications to the prayer liturgy throughout the year. For example, there are certain times of the year when additional blessings or passages are inserted into the *Shemoneh Esreh*. Because these required supplements are not represented within the *Havineinu* abridgment,[8] their utility for a person in *sha'at ha-dechak* is not obvious. Thus, one could possibly be at a loss for options in a situation where one is too encumbered to recite a full *Shemoneh Esreh*, yet where one cannot fulfill one's obligation of prayer through *Havineinu* either, because it lacks the necessary additions.

---

[8] This is only true of additions to the central thirteen blessings. If the additions are made to the first three or last three blessings, these changes are retained in *Havineinu*—which incorporates these six blessings in their entirety.

3.1 Berachot 29a—an overview

The following passage of Gemara, which details several opinions concerning the situations in which a person cannot recite *Havineinu*, follows the section of Berachot 29a discussed in the previous chapter.

תלמוד בבלי מסכת ברכות דף כט עמוד א

אמר רב נחמן אמר שמואל: כל השנה כולה מתפלל אדם הבינינו, חוץ ממוצאי שבת וממוצאי ימים טובים, מפני שצריך לומר הבדלה בחונן הדעת. מתקיף לה רבה בר שמואל: ונימרה ברכה רביעית בפני עצמה! מי לא תנן, רבי עקיבא אומר: אומרה ברכה רביעית בפני עצמה; רבי אליעזר אומר: בהודאה. אטו כל השנה כולה מי עבדינן כרבי עקיבא, דהשתא נמי נעביד? כל השנה כולה מאי טעמא לא עבדינן כרבי עקיבא - תמני סרי תקון, תשסרי לא תקון; הכא נמי - שבע תקון, תמני לא תקון. מתקיף לה מר זוטרא: ונכללה מכלל הבינונו ה' אלהינו המבדיל בין קדש לחול! קשיא.

אמר רב ביבי בר אביי: כל השנה כולה מתפלל אדם הבינונו חוץ מימות הגשמים, מפני שצריך לומר שאלה בברכת השנים. מתקיף לה מר זוטרא: ונכללה מכלל ודשננו בנאות ארץ ותן טל ומטר! אתי לאטרודי. אי הכי, הבדלה בחונן הדעת נמי אתי לאטרודי! אמרי: התם כיון דאתיא בתחלת צלותא - לא מטריד, הכא כיון דאתיא באמצע צלותא - מטריד.

Babylonian Talmud, Berachot 29a

Rav Nachman said in the name of Shmuel: Throughout the year one recites *Havineinu*, except at the conclusion of Shabbat and festivals, because one must say *Havdalah* in the blessing of *Chonein HaDa'at* (literally, Who grants wisdom; blessing of Wisdom). Rabbah bar Shmuel challenged this: let one say [*Havdalah* as] a separate fourth blessing! Does the Mishnah (Berachot 5:2) not teach, Rabbi Akiva says: one says [*Havdalah*] as a separate fourth blessing; Rabbi Eliezer says: include it in *Hoda'ah* [the blessing of Thanksgiving]? [The Gemara finds fault with Rabbah bar Shmuel's suggestion:] Is our practice throughout the year in accord with Rabbi Akiva that our practice should be that way now? Throughout the year the reason our practice is not in accordance with Rabbi Akiva is because eighteen blessings were instituted, not nineteen. Here too, seven blessings were instituted, not eight. Mar Zutra objected: let one include [*Havdalah*] among them [in *Havineinu*] by saying, "Grant us, Lord, our God, the One who distinguishes between sacred and profane, wisdom…"?! This [Mar Zutra's question] remains an [unanswered] question [on the previous opinion of Rav Nachman in the name of Shmuel].

Rav Bibi bar Abaye said: Throughout the year one recites *Havineinu*, except for the rainy season, because one must say the additional request for rain in the blessing of *Birkat HaShanim* (the blessing of 'Year of Bounty'). Mar Zutra objected: let one include [the additional request for rain] amongst them [in *Havineinu*] by saying, "Satisfy us with the products of your earth and send dew and rain?!" [A problem is found with this opinion:] One may come to be encumbered (*tarud*). If so [that encumbrance is an issue], one who adds *Havdalah* in *Chonein HaDa'at* will also come to be encumbered? They replied: there [*Havdalah*], since it comes at the beginning of the prayer, one will not be encumbered; here [rain blessing], since it comes in the middle of the prayer, one will be encumbered.

Rashi explains this passage:

רש"י מסכת ברכות דף כט עמוד א

כל השנה מי עבדינן כרבי עקיבא - כלומר: כשאנו מתפללין שמונה עשרה שלמות מי עבדינן כרבי עקיבא לומר ברכה רביעית בפני עצמה, דהשתא כשמתפללין הבינינו נעביד כותיה.

שבע תקון - שלש ראשונות ושלש אחרונות והבינינו.

ונכללה - להבדלה.

מכלל - בתוך הבינינו, כדרך שהוא כוללה בחונן הדעת, ויאמר: הבינינו ה' אלהינו המבדיל בין קדש לחול לדעת דרכיך.

לאטרודי - לטעות.

בתחלת - התפלה יכול אדם לכוין דעתו יותר מן האמצע.

Rashi, Berachot 29a

Is our practice throughout the year in accord with Rabbi Akiva? – meaning, when we recite eighteen full blessings, is our practice in accord with Rabbi Akiva to say a separate fourth blessing [for *Havdalah*], that now when we recite *Havineinu* our practice should be in accordance with his?

Seven blessings were instituted – the first three and the last three [of *Shemoneh Esreh*] and *Havineinu*.

Let one include it – *Havdalah*.

Amongst them – in *Havineinu*, in the manner that one includes it in the blessing of *Chonein HaDa'at*, and say: Grant us, Lord, our God, the One who distinguishes between sacred and profane, wisdom to understand your ways...

To be encumbered – to err.
At the beginning – of the prayer, one is better able to direct one's intention than in the middle.

This Gemara contains a complex progression of statements and refutations. (See Table 3.1 on page 74 for an outline of the argument and the following paragraphs for a summary.) It begins with a basic formulation of a rule stated by Rav Nachman in the name of Shmuel—"Throughout the year one may recite *Havineinu*, except at the conclusion of Shabbat and conclusion of festivals." The reasoning behind this ruling is that at these times, one needs to say *Havdalah* in the form of *Atah Chonantanu*[9] within the *Chonein HaDa'at* blessing. The addition of this prayer is obviously lacking from the text of the *Havineinu* abridgement. Because prayer at the conclusion of Shabbat or festivals is incomplete without this addition, *Havineinu* cannot be said at these times.

Rabbah bar Shmuel questions this assumption—even though the additional passage of *Havdalah* is missing from the *Havineinu* abridgment, why not insert the *Havdalah* prayer as a stand-alone fourth blessing? The Gemara addresses this question, debating *Havdalah*'s status as an independent blessing. The Gemara quotes a later Mishnah in Berachot (5:2) discussing where to place *Havdalah* in *Shemoneh Esreh*. Three opinions are recorded:

1. The unnamed author of the Mishnah feels that *Havdalah* should be inserted within the blessing of *Chonein HaDa'at*.
2. Rabbi Akiva maintains that *Havdalah* has the status of its own blessing within *Shemoneh Esreh*.
3. Rabbi Eliezer disagrees: one must insert *Havdalah* into the blessing of *Hoda'ah*.

The Gemara rules according to the first opinion—that *Havdalah* should be said as part of *Chonein HaDa'at*. Just as in our

---

[9] The additional passage which officially concludes the preceding Shabbat or Festival and distinguishes it from regular weekdays; it is distinct from the *Havdalah* ceremony at the conclusion of Shabbat that includes wine, spices, and a flame.

standardized version of *Shemoneh Esreh*, *Havdalah* is not its own blessing, so too *Havdalah* cannot be recited as an independent blessing within *Havineinu*. Thus, Rabbah bar Shmuel's position is rejected.

Mar Zutra offers another possible solution: One ought to be able to insert *Havdalah* into the already established *Havineinu* blessing in the position corresponding to its place in the full-length prayer. Mar Zutra proposes formulating *Havineinu*-plus-*Havdalah* as: "Grant us (*Havineinu*), Lord, our God, the One who distinguishes between sacred and profane, wisdom..." Without identifying either a logical or technical merit or flaw within Mar Zutra's suggestion, the Gemara concludes that Mar Zutra's suggestion poses a *kushya*—a difficulty—to Rav Nachman's opinion.

Leaving Rav Nachman's statement at a standstill, the Gemara picks up a similar thread, beginning with a statement by Rav Bibi bar Abaye. Like Shmuel's formulation, it begins "throughout the year one may recite *Havineinu*." However, here Rav Bibi bar Abaye makes an exception for "the rainy season" and not "the conclusion of Shabbat and festivals." During these days, one adds an extra supplication for rain called "*she'elat geshamim*." The Gemara has already rejected the possibility of adding supplemental requests as an addendum to the end of *Havineinu*, so it returns again to the second option given in the previous question—that of Mar Zutra. Parallel to his suggestion for *Chonein HaDa'at*, Mar Zutra proposes that the prayer be added in within *Havineinu*: "...build our land and give us dew and rain..."

Here the Gemara finds fault with Mar Zutra's inclusion: it is concerned with the possibility that this insertion will lead to confusion and consequently to mistakes. This concern is especially problematic for *Havineinu*, which is intended to decrease the reciter's burden and confusion. In response, the Gemara questions whether the problem of encumbrance applies to *Havdalah* as well. The Gemara answers that since *Havdalah* is inserted at the beginning of Havineinu, there will not be any confusion, unlike the rain supplement—*she'elat geshamim*—which is inserted in the middle of the prayer and therefore more likely to lead to mistakes.

Thus, *she'elat geshamim* may not be added to *Havineinu*.

Table 3.1
Content Summary of Berachot 29a

Statement	Question	Refutation
Rav Nachman in the name of Shmuel: Throughout the year one may recite *Havineinu*, except at the conclusion of Shabbat and festivals	*Rabbah bar Shmuel* asks—even though the additional prayer of *Havdalah* is missing from the *Havineinu* prayer, why not just add the *Havdalah* prayer as a fourth blessing by itself?	We have elsewhere concluded that *Havdalah* is not a separate blessing, and cannot be treated as one
	Mar Zutra proposes that *Havdalah* be added within *Havineinu*	There is no refutation— rather, it is left as a question (*kushya*)
Rav Bibi bar Abaye: Throughout the year one may recite *Havineinu*, except during the rainy season	*Mar Zutra* proposes that *she'elat geshamim* be added within *Havineinu*	One may become encumbered with this specific addition (only in the case of *she'elat geshamim*, not in the case of *Havdalah*)

Several major authorities accept both of these rulings and forbid *Havineinu* both at the conclusion of Shabbat and festivals and during the rainy season. Rambam writes:

רמב"ם הלכות תפילה ונשיאת כפים פרק ב הלכה ד

במה דברים אמורים בימות החמה, אבל בימות הגשמים אינו מתפלל הבינינו מפני שצריך לומר שאלה בברכת השנים, וכן במוצאי שבתות וימים טובים אינו מתפלל הבינינו מפני שצריך לומר הבדלה בחונן הדעת.

Rambam, Laws of Prayer 2:4

When is it the case [that one is allowed to recite *Havineinu*]? In the summer season. But in the rainy season, one may not recite *Havineinu* because one must say the additional request for rain in the blessing of 'Year of Bounty' (*Birkat HaShanim*). Similarly, at the conclusion of Shabbat and festivals, one may not recite *Havineinu*, because one must say *Havdalah* in the blessing of *Chonein HaDa'at*.

Tur concurs:

טור אורח חיים סימן קי[:א]

וכל השנה יכול להתפלל אותה חוץ מבימות הגשמים שצ"ל שאלה בברכת
השנים וחוץ ממ"ש וי"ט מפני שצ"ל הבדלה בחונן הדעת

Tur, Orach Chaim 110[:1]

Throughout the year one may recite [*Havineinu*], except in the
rainy season – because one must say the additional request for
rain in the blessing of 'Year of Bounty' (*Birkat HaShanim*), and
except at the conclusion of Shabbat and festivals – because one
must say *Havdalah* in the blessing of *Chonein HaDa'at*.

Shulchan Aruch codifies this law:

שולחן ערוך אורח חיים סימן קי:א

ואינו מתפלל הבינינו בימות הגשמים, ולא במו"ש וי"ט.

Shulchan Aruch, Orach Chaim 110:1

One may not recite *Havineinu* during the rainy season, nor at the
conclusion of Shabbat or festivals.

Rambam, Tur, and Shulchan Aruch all seem to agree with both
exceptions listed in the Gemara: *Havineinu* is a valid substitute for
every[10] *Shemoneh Esreh* except those recited at the conclusion of
Shabbat and festivals or during the rainy season. From here, it
seems that even though no official refutation was given, Mar
Zutra's proposal regarding the first exception was rejected.
However, to completely understand this approach, four questions
about this Gemara need to be addressed:

---

[10] *Shemoneh Esreh* is colloquially taken to mean the *Amidah*, the silent prayer.
Thus, the use of the term "every" is meant to include only those instances of
the *Amidah* that contain eighteen (actually nineteen) blessings, of which
Havineinu is intended as a condensation of the middle twelve (thirteen). On
some occasions, including Shabbat and festivals, the *Amidah* contains only
seven blessings. Though they have an identical opening and conclusion
(similar to *Havineinu*), the prayers on Shabbat and the festivals have their
own, day-specific, middle blessing. Because *Havineinu* is meant as an
abbreviated middle blessing and because the middle blessings are already
shorter during these specific days, *Havineinu* could not serve as a substitute
during these times.

1. Might the term "throughout the year" be so inclusive that it allows for the recitation of *Havineinu* even during non-pressing situations?
2. What could be a possible flaw with Mar Zutra's suggestion to include *Havdalah* in *Havineinu*?
3. Why is the flaw with the suggestion to insert *Havdalah* in *Havineinu* (the answer to Question Two) not raised as a concern when Mar Zutra subsequently suggests inserting *she'elat geshamim*?
4. The Gemara seems to identify a separate reason not to include *she'elat geshamim* in *Havineinu*. What precisely is this reason, and how does it differ from the objection to including *Havdalah* in *Havineinu*?

There are a number of ways to answer the questions that arise from our Gemara, and the commentators approaching these questions fall into several categories. At the extremes, there are commentators who either fully accept or fully reject Mar Zutra's position. Within this spectrum are a few commentators who only accept his inclusions with regard to *Havdalah*. Some of these commentators incorporate outside sources, while others reexamine the Gemara and completely shift the understanding of its internal, apparent flow. Many return to the original issue of *Havdalah* and revisit such issues as *sha'at ha-dechak* and the definition of "*Me'ein Shemoneh Esreh*."

Question One—Might the term "throughout the year" be so inclusive that it allows for the recitation of Havineinu *even during non-pressing situations?*

Within the context of the concepts established in the first chapter—that *Havineinu* is only permitted during *sha'at ha-dechak*, pressing circumstances—how are the statements of Rav Nachman in the name of Shmuel and Rav Bibi bar Abaye to be understood? Without any mention of *sha'at ha-dechak* or other limiting factors, they seem to imply that "throughout the year" one recites *Havineinu* in any situation. This incompatibility is easily solved if the statement, "throughout the year one recites *Havineinu*" is not understood to mean that *every day* one recites *Havineinu*, rather these are *possible* times to recite the prayer if the situations calls for it. This reading is reflected in Rabbeinu Yonah's commentary:

תלמיד רבינו יונה מסכת ברכות דף ג עמוד א
ומה שאמרו כל השנה כולה מתפלל אדם הביננו חוץ מימות הגשמים אינו
רוצה לומר בבית הכנסת אלא בדרך.

Talmid Rabbeinu Yonah, Berachot 3a
And that which the Talmud said, "Throughout the year one
recites *Havineinu* except for the rainy season," it did not mean to
say in the synagogue—but rather on the road.

Rather than implying that every day one *must*—or even ought
to—recite *Havineinu*, the Gemara outlines that "throughout the
year" one is *permitted* to recite *Havineinu*. Mindful of the
stipulation of *sha'at ha-dechak*, Rabbeinu Yonah clarifies what is
considered to be a "permitted" situation. "Throughout the year"
does not apply when praying in the synagogue (the prime
example of an un-pressured situation), but only when traveling
on the road (which can be interpreted as a time of *dechak*.) This
restriction is accepted by a great many authorities.

*Question Two— What could be a possible flaw with Mar Zutra's
suggestion to include* Havdalah *in* Havineinu?

An obvious point of disagreement among readers of this Gemara
is over the outcome of Mar Zutra's challenge to the two
statements proscribing *Havineinu* at the conclusion of Shabbat and
festivals and during the rainy season—particularly the first,
which is left unanswered in the Gemara. One approach is taken
by Rambam, Tur, and Shulchan Aruch, who all rule against Mar
Zutra in favor of Rav Nachman's and Rav Bibi's opinions. These
rulings raise the question of why Mar Zutra's suggestion of
modifying the *Havineinu* text, while remaining undisputed in the
Gemara, is not accepted as halacha.

Mar Zutra is consistent. In the cases of both *Havdalah* and *she'elat
geshamim*, he suggests additions within the *Havineinu* prayer.
However, two very different responses to his identical challenges
are found. Concerning *she'elat geshamim*, the Gemara refers to the
difficulties of this inclusion (which will be discussed at greater
length in the next section). Conversely, in the case of *Havdalah*,

Mar Zutra's objection is left unanswered. The Gemara admits that
Mar Zutra's question raises a legitimate difficulty (*kushya*) to the
previous opinions, yet offers no refutation of his position. Though
to some, this wording seems to imply a default acceptance of Mar
Zutra's opinion, a significant group of commentators disagree.
While the Gemara does not offer an answer to Mar Zutra's
question, these commentators do—implying a flaw in Mar Zutra's
suggestion. The basis for their further ability to suggest an answer
to the question is in a careful reading of the wording of the
Gemara. Despite the seemingly clear lack of a resolution to his
difficult question (*kushya*), Mar Zutra's challenge does not
necessarily have the full force of a refutation (*tiyuvta*) against Rav
Nachman's position. Therefore, Rambam, Tur, and Shulchan
Aruch's rejection of Mar Zutra's suggestion is legitimate. Rashba
elaborates on this reasoning:

חידושי הרשב"א מסכת ברכות דף כט עמוד א

מתקיף לה מר זוטרא ונכללה מכלל הבינינו ה' אלהינו המבדיל בין קודש
לחול *קשיא* - וכתב הגאון ר"ה ז"ל דאע"ג דסלקא בקושיא לא מדחי' הא
דר"נ דאמר משמיה דשמואל כיון דלא סלקא בתיובתא אלא בקושיי'
דדילמא אי עיינינן בה משכחינן לה פירוקא ומשום קושיא לא דחי' לה,
והלכך לא מצלינן הבינינו במוצאי שבתות ובמוצאי י"ט

Rashba, Berachot 29a

Mar Zutra objected: let one include [Havdalah] in Havineinu *by
saying, Grant us, Lord, our God, the One who distinguishes between
sacred and profane, wisdom. This remains a question –* And Rav Hai
Gaon of blessed memory wrote that even though the Talmud
concluded with an unresolved question, the ruling of Rav
Nachman in the name of Shmuel was not rejected, because the
Talmud did not conclude with a term of definitive refutation
(*tiyuvta*), but rather with a strong question (*kushya*)—for perhaps
if we were to examine the matter further, we would find a
suitable resolution. Thus, from the force of a [mere] strong
difficulty, we do not reject the ruling. Therefore we do not recite
Havineinu at the conclusion of Shabbat or festivals.

Rashba, in the name of Rav Hai Gaon, focuses on the wording of
the Gemara: "there is a difficulty (*kushya*)." Even though the
Gemara considers Mar Zutra's question on Shmuel to be a
difficulty, the idea remains a possibility, it is not a full "refutation"

(*tiyuvta*) of Shmuel's statement.

While Rashba leaves open the possibility for a response to Mar Zutra, he does not provide one. Rabbeinu Yonah, however, addresses the open question differently. He identifies a potential problem that would arise from Mar Zutra's proposal. Because *Havdalah* is not considered a stand-alone blessing of the *Shemoneh Esreh*, it cannot be treated as one. Although Mar Zutra's suggestion does not technically violate this rule, it does produce a misconception about the classification of *Havdalah* as a blessing.

תלמיד ר' יונה ברכות כט עמוד א (יט עמוד ב בדפי הרי"ף)

מפני שצריך לומר *הבדלה בחונן הדעת* – ובגמרא (דף כט [עמוד] א)
שואל כמו שאומר מעין כל ברכה וברכה משמנה עשרה למה אינו אומר
ג"כ מעין הבדלה ויתפלל הביננו אפי' במוצ"ש ובמוצאי ימים טובים
ונשאר בקושיא ואפ"ה מילתיה דשמואל הלכתא הוי ואפשר לומר טעם
בדבר דמשום הכי לא תקינו מעין הבדלה מפני שההבדלה אינה ברכה
בפני עצמה אלא שאנו כוללים אותה בברכת אתה חונן ואם היו אומרים
מעין הבדלה היה נראה שההבדלה היא ברכה בפני עצמה כיון שהתקינו
מעין הבדלה כמו שתקנו מעין שאר ברכות:

Talmid Rabbeinu Yonah, Berachot 29a (19b in Rif pagination)
Because one must say Havdalah in the blessing of Chonein HaDa'at –
The Talmud (Berachot 29a) asks, just as one says an abstraction of each and every blessing, why not say an abstraction of *Havdalah* as well, and recite *Havineinu* even at the conclusion of Shabbat and festivals? The Talmud concludes with the question unresolved. Nevertheless, the ruling of Shmuel remains the law. Perhaps one could offer a reason for this, that for the following reason [the Sages] did not institute an abstraction of *Havdalah*: *Havdalah* is not an independent blessing; rather, it is included in the blessing of *Atah Chonein* (Who grants wisdom)—but were we to allow an abstraction of *Havdalah*, it would appear as if *Havdalah* were an independent blessing, since [the sages] instituted an abstraction of *Havdalah* just as they instituted an abstraction of the other blessings.

Before addressing the potential difficulties that arise from Mar Zutra's suggestion, Rabbeinu Yonah reiterates the following proposition. If *Havineinu* is an abridgement of the entire *Shemoneh Esreh*, why not shorten the *Havdalah* insertion as well and add it into the prayer? Because, he answers, if *Havdalah* were reduced into

Havineinu like all the other blessings are, it might appear to some that the *Havdalah* addition has the status of an independent blessing. Although Rabbeinu Yonah outlines the potential misconception that could develop by implementing Mar Zutra's proposal, he does not address the consequences of such an error. It is also unclear within what context this concern applies—will the incorrect treatment of *Havdalah* as a blessing affect the validity of the recitation of *Havineinu* or *Shemoneh Esreh*? Addressing these concerns, Bach explores the ramifications of considering *Havdalah* to be a separate blessing. Bach notes that in reality, no one is likely to become confused about the structure of *Havdalah* (as implied by Rabbeinu Yonah's commentary), since everyone knows that in the full *Shemoneh Esreh*, *Havdalah* is included in the blessing of *Chonein HaDa'at*. Rather, it is the laws regarding the addition of *Havdalah* into *Shemoneh Esreh* that are affected. Specifically, the concern is that someone might think that the laws of the individual blessings are equally applicable to *Havdalah*. Thus, Bach concludes that the concern with conceiving of *Havdalah* as a separate blessing applies to the laws—not the structure—of *Shemoneh Esreh* or *Havineinu*.

ב"ח אורח חיים קי:ב

וכתב ה"ר יונה אע"ג דאסיקנא בקשיא מילתא דשמואל לא אידחיא ואפשר לתרץ הקושיא שאם היו אומרים מעין הבדלה וכוללים אותה בהבינינו היה נראה שההבדלה היא ברכה בפני עצמה כיון שהתקינו [מעין הבדלה כמו שתקנו] מעין שאר ברכות עכ"ל:

ותימה דמה לנו לחוש אם היה נראה שהיא ברכה בפני עצמה הא ודאי דלא מפני שהיה נראה כך יקבעו להבדלה ברכה בפני עצמה כרבי עקיבא במשנה פרק אין עומדין (ברכות לג.) דכבר נהגו לכוללה בחונן הדעת ויש לומר שחוששין שמתוך שהיא נראה שהיא ברכה בפני עצמה יבואו לומר שדין הבדלה כדין שאר ברכות שמונה עשרה דאם שכח ולא אמרה מחזירין אותו ויברכו ברכה לבטלה...

Bach, Orach Chaim 110:2

Rabbeinu Yonah wrote that even though the Talmud concluded with an unresolved question (*kushya*), the ruling of Shmuel was not rejected—and moreover, that it might be possible to resolve this question by saying that if we were to allow one to say an abstraction of *Havdalah* and include it in *Havineinu*, it would appear as if *Havdalah* were an independent blessing, since [the sages] instituted an abstraction of *Havdalah* just as they instituted an abstraction of the other blessings.

But this poses a difficulty – for why should we be concerned that [*Havdalah*] would appear to be an independent blessing? It certainly cannot mean that it would appear that the sages instituted that *Havdalah* be a separate blessing in accordance with Rabbi Akiva in the Mishnah in the fifth chapter of Berachot, for the practice had already been accepted to include *Havdalah* [in the full *Shemoneh Esreh*] in the blessing of *Chonein HaDa'at*! One may respond by saying that we are concerned that since [*Havdalah*] would appear to be a separate blessing [in *Havineinu*], one would [incorrectly] conclude that the rule for *Havdalah* is akin to the rule for the other blessings in *Shemoneh Esreh*: if one forgets to say the blessing, one repeats the entire [*Shemoneh Esreh*]—this would lead to people making blessings in vain. (Continued below)

Bach explains that the problem with considering *Havdalah* a separate blessing is the resulting misconception about the laws of mistakenly forgotten blessings within *Shemoneh Esreh*. While with all blessings that are mistakenly omitted from *Shemoneh Esreh* one is obligated to repeat the entire prayer, the situation is different with regard to *Havdalah*. If one omits *Atah Chonantanu*, there is no obligation to repeat the *Shemoneh Esreh*. Furthermore, doing so would be considered a blessing recited in vain, which is forbidden. This is why, Bach concludes, *Havdalah* cannot be included in the *Havineinu* prayer. From the misconception that *Havdalah* is its own blessing, one might develop the false notion that one is obligated to repeat the entire *Shemoneh Esreh* if *Havdalah* were omitted. (The above views are summarized in Table 3.2.)

Question Three—Why is the flaw with Mar Zutra's suggestion to insert Havdalah *in* Havineinu *(the answer to Question Two) not raised as a concern when he subsequently suggests inserting she'elat geshamim?*

Although not specified in the Gemara, developing a misconception could be a direct result of following Mar Zutra's suggestion of adding *Havdalah* in as a separate blessing. Why then does the possiblity of misconception not apply to *she'elat geshamim* (as evidenced by the Gemara giving an alternate answer to Mar Zutra's question)? Bach continues his commentary and explains:

Table 3.2
Flow of Ideas: the answer to Mar Zutra's question on *Havdalah*

Gemara

Rav Nachman in the name of Shmuel: One may not say *Havineinu* at the conclusion of Shabbat and festivals because there is an addition to include, *Havdalah,* which is not found in *Havineinu.*

Mar Zutra: Why not just include *Havdalah* as an additional abridgment?

Gemara: Mar Zutra's question remains unresolved.

Commentaries

Rashba: We do not accept Mar Zutra's challenge as a bona fide refutation.

Rabbeinu Yonah: This is because we are concerned that one will develop the misconception that *Havdalah* is its own blessing.

Bach: This would lead one to misconstrue the law concerning the need to repeat *Shemoneh Esreh* when one forgets to add *Havdalah.*

ב"ח אורח חיים קי:ב (המשך)

ובהכי ניחא דדחיק תלמודא גבי שאלה וקא משני דהא דאין כוללין אותה בהבינינו היינו משום דאתא למיטרד ולמיטעי ולא קאמר האי טעמא דהיה נראה שהיא ברכה בפני עצמה אלא דלפי דגבי שאלה אין לנו לחוש לזה שיהיה נראה להם דהשאלה היא ברכה בפני עצמה ויבואו לומר דאם שכח מלאומרה דמחזירין אותו דהא קושטא הכי הוא דאם טעה ולא אמר שאלה בברכת השנים מחזירין.

Bach, Orach Chaim, 110:2 (continued)

And this helps to explain why the Talmud gave a separate answer with regard to the additional prayer for rain and explained that the reason that one does not include it in *Havineinu* is because one will come to be encumbered and err, and it did not suggest that it would appear as if it were an independent blessing: because regarding the additional prayer for rain, we need not be concerned that it would appear to be an independent blessing such that people would conclude that if one forgot to say it one must repeat [the entire *Shemoneh Esreh*]— for this is indeed correct! For if one erred and did not add the request for rain in 'Year of Bounty' (*Birkat HaShanim*), one must return [to the beginning of the *Shemoneh Esreh*].

Unlike forgetting *Havdalah* in tefillah, for which one is not obligated to repeat *Shemoneh Esreh*, omitting *she'elat geshamim* does require one to repeat the *Shemoneh Esreh*. Therefore, no practical ramifications exist from a potential misconception about the role of the rain supplication. If one were to mistakenly consider it a separate blessing and therefore conclude that the entire *Shemoneh Esreh* must be repeated if forgotten, one would not err in practice. (See Table 3.3.)

Table 3.3
Summary of laws involving *Havdalah* and seasonal request for rain

Addition	Where added into *Shemoneh Esreh*	What to do if one forgets addition	Does it make a practical difference if a misconception develops?
Havdalah (in form of *Atah Chonantanu*)	*Chonein HaDa'at*	Do not repeat *Shemoneh Esreh*	Yes
She'elat geshamim (rain supplication)	*Birkat HaShanim*	Repeat *Shemoneh Esreh*	No

Whereas Rav Hai Gaon (as quoted by Rashba) maintains that the Gemara concludes by not accepting Mar Zutra on the basis that "...perhaps if we were to examine the matter further, we would find a suitable resolution," Bach's commentary suggests that he would say that the Gemara actually *had this entire construction in mind* throughout the discussion. Otherwise, there would be no need to explain why the Talmud gave a different answer for *she'elat geshamim*. By contrast, according to the usual understanding of Rav Hai Gaon, the answer is simple: the Gemara didn't know the answer—it just identified a strong question and trusted in the possibility of an answer.

Perishah elaborates on this distinction from a different angle. While Bach explains why there is no harm if one mistakes the *she'elat geshamim* for an independent blessing, Perishah shows why this type of misconception is unlikely to occur. Because the text of *Havdalah* (the separator between holy and profane) has little thematic connection to the blessing in conjunction with which it is said, *"Chonein HaDa'at* ('You grant wisdom'), it could easily be falsely perceived as a separate blessing. This would not be true with *"ve-tein tal umatar"* (the rain supplication), because its theme is closely tied to its contextual blessing, *Birkat HaShanim* ('Year of Bounty').

פרישה אורח חיים קי:ד

וחוץ ממוצאי שבת- ... והר"י נתן טעם מפני שהיה נראה שהבדלה היא ברכה בפני עצמה ואינה ברכה בפני עצמה אלא דינה לכוללה בברכת אתה חונן עכ"ל וקצת קשה למה זה אמר לא הטעם גם כן בשאלה והיה נראה דדוקא בהבדלה שאינו ענין לברכת אתה חונן היה נחשב לברכה בפני עצמה מה שאין כן ותן טל ומטר שהוא מעין ודשננו בנאות ארצך...

Perishah, Orach Chaim 110:4

And except for the conclusion of Shabbat – ... Rabbeinu Yonah suggested a reason [why *Havdalah* cannot be inserted *Havineinu*], that because it would appear as if *Havdalah* were an independent blessing, but it is not an independent blessing; rather, the rule is that one should include it [*Havdalah*] in *Atah Chonein*.

This seems somewhat difficult: why was this reason not given regarding the additional prayer for rain? It would seem [the answer is] that particularly with regard to *Havdalah*, which is not related to the topic of the blessing of wisdom, would one think [the insertion] to represent an independent blessing—as opposed to an insertion for the additional prayer for rain (*ve-tein tal umatar*), which *does* closely relate to the topic of "bring produce forth from the land." [Emphasis added] (Continued below, in discussion of Question Four.)

Perishah does not deal with the (practical) ramifications of misconception, but rather with the likelihood that it will occur. If there is no concern about potential misconception about *She'elat Geshamim*—with regard to its impact on the law or as a result of its thematic contact—what is the difficulty with including it into the *Havineinu* as Mar Zutra suggests? Following this logic, *Havdalah* should be excluded from *Havineinu*, yet *she'elat geshamim* should be permitted to be inserted.

Question Four— The Gemara seems to identify a separate reason not to include she'elat geshamim *in* Havineinu. *What precisely is this reason, and how does it differ from the objection to including* Havdalah *in* Havineinu?

The Gemara itself raises a difficulty with Mar Zutra's suggestion to include an abstraction of *she'elat geshamim* in *Havineinu*: A person might become encumbered (confused or burdened) when required to insert a special addition in the middle of a prayer.

Rashi elaborates upon the view of the Gemara about the greater potential of confusion as a prayer proceeds:

רש"י מסכת ברכות דף כט עמוד א
בתחלת - התפלה יכול אדם לכוין דעתו יותר מן האמצע.
Rashi, Berachot 29a
At the beginning – of the prayer, one is better able to direct one's intention than in the middle.

Rashi identifies a connection between the location within prayer and the level of concentration: it is harder to focus and remember to insert a supplement during the middle of a prayer (for *she'elat geshamim*) than at the beginning of the prayer (for the *Havdalah* addition.)

Many commentators, including Bach and Beit Yosef, adopt this position. Mar Zutra's challenges are both refuted—the *Havdalah* insertion results in misconception, while *she'elat geshamim* involves encumbrance. (See summary in Table 3.4.)

At first glance, the Gemara's reasoning (and Rashi's interpretation) appears problematic. Mar Zutra's proposal to insert an addition for the rainy season is rejected because inserting an addition into the middle of the prayer might cause confusion. Yet, in the full *Shemoneh Esreh, she'elat geshamim* is similarly inserted into *Birkat HaShanim* with no concern for the possibility of confusion. Sensitive to this problem, while defining "*tarud*," Beit Yosef and Bach resolve this inconsistency:

Table 3.4
Additions to *Shemoneh Esreh* and their implications for *Havineinu*

Halachic Facts			Rationale
Addition	**Where Added**	**If Forgotten**	**Reason for not including in *Havineinu***
Havdalah (in form of *Atah Chonantanu*)	*Chonein HaDa'at* (found at beginning of *Shemoneh Esreh*)	Do not repeat *Shemoneh Esreh*	Misconception (Rabbeinu Yonah)
She'elat Geshamim (Rain supplication)	*Birkat HaShanim* (found in middle of *Shemoneh Esreh*)	Repeat *Shemoneh Esreh*	Encumbrance (Gemara)

בית יוסף אורח חיים סימן קי[:א]

...ומשני אתי לאיטרודי כלומר לטעות ונראה לי דהא דחייישינן שיטעה
יותר בתפילת הבינינו מבתפילת י"ח הוא מפני שאדם עשוי לטעות ביותר
בדברים קצרים שבקל אדם יכול לדלג שתים או שלש תיבות או להוסיף
אותם:

Beit Yosef, Orach Chaim 110[:1]
...The Talmud answers that one will come to be encumbered—
meaning, to err. And it seems to me that the concern that one
will more likely err in *Havineinu* than in the full *Shemoneh Esreh*
is because a person is more likely to err in shorter passages
where one may easily omit two or three words or [incorrectly]
add them.

Beit Yosef explains that due to the brevity of *Havineinu*, it is easy
to err and accidentally add a few words—because one would be
so familiar with the usual expanded text—or omit a few words—
because one does not know *Havineinu* well enough. Note that Beit
Yosef's definition of "encumbered" relates to the potential for
textual error.

ב"ח אורח חיים קי:ב

וכתב בית יוסף אהא דקאמר אתי לאטרודי פירוש לטעות וצריך לומר
דהא דחייישינן שיטעה יותר בתפילת הבינינו מבתפילת י"ח הוא מפני
שאדם עשוי לטעות ביותר בדברים קצרים שנקל לאדם לדלג שתים או
שלש תיבות או להוסיף אותם עכ"ל. נראה שהבין שתלמודא הכי קאמר

דאתי לטעות וידלג שתים או שלש תיבות ותימה דאם כן אמאי חיישינן
טפי דכשבא לכלול השאלה בברכת הבינינו דאתי לדלג בלאו שאלה נמי
אתי לדלג שתים או שלש תיבות ויהיה הבינינו חסר ברכה אחת מן
האמצעיות. אלא ודאי לא חיישינן לדילוג אלא חיישינן דמתוך שהם
דברים קצרים שמא יהא טועה שלא יהא כולל ותן טל ומטר אצל ודשננו
בנאות ארץ אלא למעלה ממנו או למטה ממנו ואנן בעינן שאלה בברכת
השנים אבל בתפילת י"ח יודע את מקומה בברכת השנים שהיא ברכה
ארוכה ואין לטעות בקביעות ותן טל ומטר למעלה ממנה או למטה ממנה
ופשוט הוא:

Bach, Orach Chaim 110:2

Beit Yosef wrote regarding that which [the Talmud] says, one
will come to be encumbered: "Meaning, to err, and one must say
that the concern that one will more likely err in *Havineinu* than in
the full *Shemoneh Esreh* is because a person is more likely to err in
shorter passages where one may easily omit two or three words
or [incorrectly] add them." It appears that he understood the
Talmud to say as follows: [that if one were to be able to add
she'elat geshamim in *Havineinu*,] one would come to err and omit
two or three words. But this seems difficult—[because] if so,
why are we more concerned when one comes to include the
additional prayer for rain in *Havineinu* than that one will come to
omit words—even without the addition for rain (*she'elat
geshamim*) one could come to omit one or two words of [the
short] *Havineinu* which will result in an incomplete *Havineinu*
that is missing a blessing. Rather, we are certainly not concerned
about omission; we are instead concerned that since [*Havineinu*]
is a short passage, perhaps one will err and not include the line
"grant us dew and rain" immediately after "satisfy us with the
products of your earth," but rather someplace before or after—
but the law requires the addition for rain to be made at that
particular point. However, in the full *Shemoneh Esreh*, one knows
its proper place in the blessing of *Birkat HaShanim* ('Year of
Bounty') which is a lengthy blessing and one would not err in
setting the addition for rain [in a blessing] before or after—this is
obvious.

Bach disagrees with Beit Yosef. If it is the brief nature of *Havineinu*
which causes confusion, then the entire prayer of *Havineinu*
becomes problematic. Therefore Bach alters Beit Yosef's
formulation, explaining that it is the brief nature of the *Havineinu*
coupled with trying to remember the specifics of where to add the
supplementary phrase ("before or after") that results in confusion.

Thus, Bach defines "encumbered" as the possibility of transposing the text and not simply as skipping words.

Beit Yosef views the Gemara's final concern as the addition or omission of words, whereas Bach sees the concern as one of erroneous textual placement. They also both follow the reading of Rabbeinu Yonah, which states that the problem with inserting *Havdalah* into *Havineinu* is the potential for misconception with regard to the *Shemoneh Esreh*. This seems to be the position of the majority of the commentators, but there are a few innovative perspectives which take a different view.

Innovative perspectives; diverging from the current approach

All the commentaries cited thus far have subscribed to Bach's understanding of Rabbeinu Yonah's reasoning concerning the problem of inserting *Havdalah* into *Havineinu;* they recognize that this practice might create a misconception that *Havdalah* is its own blessing. However, not all commentaries take this viewpoint. Consider the views of Rashba, Perishah and Tosafot. Rashba does not take Rabbeinu Yonah's approach to the Gemara's *kushya* into account. In a departure from most of the commentators mentioned, Rashba accepts Mar Zutra's first challenge in the Gemara—allowing the recitation of *Havineinu* at the conclusion of Shabbat and festivals. Not as radical in practice, yet a true act of intellectual acrobatics, Perishah reads the Gemara's give-and-take innovatively. He claims that the final questioner recorded in the Gemara "misunderstood" a point of his predecessors, leading to something of a non sequitur in the Talmudic passage. Tosafot develop the *halacha* further by incorporating another Gemara into their reading. Their analysis will enable others, such as Ravad, to make novel interpretations regarding the *Havineinu* practice.

Twice—at the initial proposal of *Havdalah's* conclusion and when a distinction is drawn between the *Havdalah* insertion and *she'elat geshamim*—the Gemara finds no difficulty with Mar Zutra's suggested inclusion of *Havdalah* into *Havineinu*. Rashba, representing a minority approach, interprets the Gemara's lack of response to Mar Zutra in the case of *Havdalah* as a proof that Mar Zutra's challenge is accepted.

חידושי הרשב"א מסכת ברכות דף כט עמוד א

ומסתברא דאפילו במוצאי שבתות וי"ט דרב ביבי בר אביי דהוא בתרא
קאמר כל השנה מתפלל אדם הביננו חוץ מימות הגשמים ודוקא חוץ
מימות הגשמים קאמר ואפילו במוצאי שבתות וימים טובים וכדמשמע
ממאי דאתקיף עליה מר זוטרא ונכלליה מכלל ודשננו בנאות ארצך ותן
טל ומטר ופריק דילמא אתי לאטרודי ואקשינן אי הכי הבדלה בחונן הדעת
אתי לאיטרודי אמרי כיון דבתחלת צלותיה לא מטריד אלמא לרב ביבי
אפי' במוצאי שבתות וי"ט אמרי' ליה, וה"ר יצחק בר"י בן גיאת ז"ל הכין
פסק כאתקפתא דמר זוטרא, ומיהו בימות הגשמים משמע דלא מצלי לה
דהא פריק מאי דאקשי עליה מר זוטרא דכיון דבאמצע צלותיה הוא אתי
לאטרודי.

Rashba, Berachot 29a
One might logically deduce that one may recite *Havineinu* even
at the conclusion of Shabbat or festivals, for Rav Bibi bar Abaye,
who was the latter sage, ruled that throughout the year one may
recite *Havineinu* except for the rainy season—he meant to
particularly exclude the rainy season [and nothing else], even the
conclusion of Shabbat and festivals. This may also be inferred
from [the underlying assumptions of the Talmudic passage itself,
where] Mar Zutra objects: let one include [the additional prayer
for rain] by saying, "satisfy us with the products of your earth
and send dew and rain," and the Talmud responds, perhaps one
will come to be encumbered. The Talmud then asks, if so, one
who adds *Havdalah* in [the place for the blessing of] *Chonein
HaDa'at* will also come to be encumbered? They answer: since it
comes at the beginning of one's prayer, one will not be
encumbered. We see from this that according to Rav Bibi, one
does recite *Havineinu* at the conclusion of Shabbat and festivals.
And R. Isaac ben R. Yehudah ibn Ghayyat [c.1030–1089] of
blessed memory ruled in accordance with the [first] objection of
Mar Zutra; however, it seems that during the rainy season one
may not recite *Havineinu*, for the Talmud responded to the
[second] question of Mar Zutra by saying that since the
additional prayer for rain occurs in the middle of one's prayer,
one will indeed become encumbered.

Rashba examines the flow of the Gemara. It begins, "throughout
the year one may recite *Havineinu*"; adds a caveat, "except for the
conclusion of Shabbat and festivals"; and then neither accepts nor
rejects this stipulation. Another general statement is then made,
"throughout the year one may recite *Havineinu*," which most

interpret to be the beginning of a new line of thought. Rashba, though, interprets this phrase as a tacit acceptance of Mar Zutra's inclusion. Thus, the second section of the Gemara should be understood as reading, "throughout the year—*including the conclusion of Shabbat and festivals*—one may recite *Havineinu*, but not during the rainy season." Rashba finds support for this reading in the second section of the Gemara's treatment of *Havdalah*. The Gemara states that saying the *Havdalah* insertion in *Havieninu* will not encumber a person, implying that this practice is permissible. Although not explicitly stated, it can be assumed that Rashba rules against Rabbeinu Yonah's reading in his commentary: "We see from this that according to Rav Bibi, one *does* say *Havineinu* at the conclusion of Shabbat and festivals." (See Table 3.5.)

The progression of the Gemara seems to support, not reject, Mar Zutra's inclusions. Perishah's earlier comments—that the *Havdalah* insertion is thematically unrelated to its context, and thus there is a greater potential for misconception concerning *Havdalah* than *she'elat geshamim*—are in accordance with Rabbeinu Yonah's assumption that adding *Havdalah* into *Havineinu* results in misconception. However, Perishah challenges his own explanation based on the text of the Gemara itself. While Perishah's explanation seems logically sound and works to explain the language of *kushya* rather than *tiyuvta* in the first part of the Gemara, it does not work well with the rest of the Gemara. Indeed, an alternative answer appears, implying that Perishah's construct is not valid. The Gemara's refutation of Mar Zutra's suggestion with regard to *she'elat geshamim* does not address *Havdalah*—making the Gemara's earlier lack of response (*kushya*) even stronger. Perishah understands this weakness and addresses it:

פרישה אורח חיים קי:ד, ד"ה: וחוץ ממוצאי שבת (המשך)

...אך קשה דאם כן הוא היה לתלמודא לומר תירוץ זה ומדלא אמרה ודאי
לא סבירא ליה לתלמודא האי סברא למיחש ואפשר לומר שהמתרץ
כשהשיב לו מתחלה דילמא אתי לאיטרודי היתה כוונתו לומר שמא יטרד
פעם אחרת ויחשבנה לברכה בפני עצמה ולא כסברת ר' יונה ולא היה
חושש שיטרד וידלג אך שהמקשן סליק אדעתיה שהשיב לו טירדות של

Table 3.5
View of Rashba compared to Bach and Beit Yosef

Halachic Facts			Commentaries' explanation of reason this addition can or cannot be made to *Havineinu*	
Addition	**Where Added**	**If Forgotten**	**Bach/Beit Yosef**	**Rashba**
Havdalah	*Atah Chonantanu*	Do not repeat *Shemoneh Esreh*	Misconception— people will think it is a blessing on its own (Rabbeinu Yonah)	*May* be inserted into *Havineinu* (There is no problem)
She'elat Geshamim	*Birkat HaShanim*	Repeat *Shemoneh Esreh*	Encumbrance (Gemara) Beit Yosef: adding/omitting words Bach: mis-placement of words	Encumbrance (because it's in the middle of the prayer)

דילוג והתרצן הואיל וידע האי האי שינויא לרוב פשטותו בעיניו לא חש
להשיב על אתקפתא בתרייתא וק"ל:

Perishah, Orach Chaim 110:4 (continued)

However, a difficulty remains [with my previously suggested answer that particularly with regard to *Havdalah*, which is not related to the topic of the blessing of wisdom, would one think (the insertion) to represent an independent blessing—as opposed to an insertion for the additional prayer for rain (*ve-tein tal umatar*), which *does* closely relate to the topic of "bring produce forth from the land."]: for were this in fact the case, the Talmud should have given that answer [in reply to Mar Zutra], but by the fact that it did not, the Talmud was clearly not concerned about this possibility. Perhaps one could answer, then, that [the unnamed Talmudic sage (Amora)] who answered [Mar Zutra] saying, "One might come to be encumbered," intended to say that perhaps one would come to be encumbered at a later time [when reciting *Shemoneh Esreh*] and consider [the additional prayer for rain] to be an independent blessing—unlike the reasoning of Rabbeinu Yonah [who thought that the issue of being considered an independent blessing was not relevant to the additional prayer for rain]—and [that Amora] was not concerned with the issue of becoming encumbered [at this time—during *Havineinu*] or omitting [the necessary insertion]. However, the next unnamed Amora who asked a question on this [additions cause problems] position believed the [previous] answer to mean that one might come to be encumbered and omit [the necessary insertion into *Havineinu*]. The first Amora who had given the answer—since he understood that teaching to be most simply correct—never concerned himself with answering the latter objection.

Perishah, like Tur on whom he comments, does not include the *Havdalah* addition in *Havineinu*. This ruling shows that Perishah has a legitimate response to Mar Zutra's suggestions, and Perishah must find a way to read the Gemara so that his own answer still stands. His first attempt, quoted previously in this chapter, was to accept Rabbeinu Yonah's recognition of potential misconception. However, Perishah himself finds fault with this approach—why does the second section of the Gemara not recognize this aspect of the additions when mentioning the problems involved in incorporating additions into *Havineinu*? To resolve this problem, Perishah explains that the two sections are in fact talking about different issues. Thus, it is understandable why the proposed answer is not brought up within both sections of the Gemara—it only applies to one of them. The different approaches are dealing with misconception, encumbrance and error within specific contexts—*Havineinu* and *Shemoneh Esreh*.

As Perishah explains, adding *Havdalah* into *Havineinu* results in a misconception within **Shemoneh Esreh**. Accordingly, Perishah offers an explanation (based on thematic content) with regard to *Shemoneh Esreh*. Although the segment of the Gemara discussing *she'elat geshamim* also deals with encumbrance in **Shemoneh Esreh**, the response to this difficulty is dealing with **Havineinu**. Thus, because it is dealing with a different subject altogether, there is no contradiction.

By reading the Gemara in the following way, Perishah avoids any internal contradiction in the Gemara:

Statement of first Amora	*Premise*: [If one were allowed to add *she'elat geshamim* to *Havineinu*]
	Conclusion: **one may come to be encumbered [in** *SHEMONEH ESREH*].
Question of second Amora	*(Incorrect) understanding of prior statement*: If so [were one allowed to add *she'elat geshamim* to *Havineinu*, and therefore] **one may come to be encumbered [in** *HAVINEINU*],
	Question: then one who adds *Havdalah* in the [the blessing of] *Chonein HaDa'at* will also **come to be encumbered [in** *HAVINEINU*]?

Notice that according to Perishah's reading of the Gemara, the question asked by the second Amora shows a misunderstanding of the initial statement. Because the question segment of this dialogue is asking an unrelated question, it is invalid as a proof that *Havdalah* is the accepted prayer. Table 3.6 shows the difference between Perishah's reading, and the commentators presented in the previous sections.

Perishah interprets both insertions to lead to difficulties not in *Havineinu*, but in *Shemoneh Esreh*. What would lead Perishah to think that this prayer, relegated for use only in extreme situations, would ever influence the instituted prayer *Shemoneh Esreh*? Perhaps, it is the underlying assumption that there is a higher familiarity with *Havineinu* than with *Shemoneh Esreh*. When reciting *Havineinu* is someone's norm, and a full *Shemoneh Esreh* then becomes the exception, instead of basing the text of *Havineinu* on *Shemoneh Esreh*, the reverse would occur: the text of *Shemoneh Esreh* would be derived from the more familiar *Havineinu* prayer. In such a case, the danger of inserting *Havdalah* into *Havineinu* would be the potential encumbrance upon reciting the full *Shemoneh Esreh*.

Table 3.6
Berachot 29a as understood by Perishah

Gemara		Where this concern applies	
Problem	Reaction	Approach presented in previous section	Perishah
May *Havdalah* be inserted into *Havineinu*?	*Kushya* Some take this to mean that it may be included; others rule that it may not, due to the potential for misconception	*Shemoneh Esreh*	*Shemoneh Esreh*
May *she'elat geshamim* be inserted into *Havineinu*?	No, due to potential for encumbrance	*Havineinu*	*Shemoneh Esreh*
Why does encumbrance not apply to *Havdalah*?	There is no issue of encumbrance at the beginning of prayer	*Havineinu*	The Amora who asked the question is doing so on the premise that the previous statement was made about *Havineinu*

The Gemara in Tractate Niddah

Rashba's reading of the Gemara is notably different from other readings: he accepts Mar Zutra's *Havdalah* inclusion. Tosafot may have a similar conclusion to Rashba, but their interpretive methods are divergent. Rashba focuses on the nuances of the flow within the Gemara in Berachot, while Tosafot incorporate another Gemara from Tractate Niddah.

Thus far encumbrance (burden) and misconception have been cited as the primary reasons that *Havineinu* cannot be recited at the conclusion of Shabbat and festivals. At the conclusion of Yom Kippur, when burden would become a significant issue because of the fast, the need for *Havineinu* is great. Yet, the Gemara in Niddah seems to insist that *Shemoneh Esreh* must be recited. Evidently, *Havineinu* is not able to be said at this time because of the required inclusion:

תלמוד בבלי מסכת נדה דף ח עמוד ב

רבי חנינא בן גמליאל משום אבותיו אומר: מתפלל שמנה עשרה, מפני שצ"ל הבדלה בחונן הדעת.

Babylonian Talmud, Niddah 8b

Rabbi Chanina ben Gamliel said in the name of his ancestors: One must recite the full eighteen blessings (*Shemoneh Esreh*) [at the conclusion of Yom Kippur] because one must include *Havdalah* in the blessing of *Chonein HaDa'at*.

Tosafot, however, do not view this omission as a proof that *Havineinu* is a rejected alternative for the conclusion of Shabbat and festivals. Rather, they argue:

תוספות מסכת ברכות דף כט עמוד א

ונכללה בהביננו—והא דאמרינן בפ"ק דנדה (דף ח:) כל השנה כולה מתפלל אדם י"ח חוץ ממוצאי יה"כ מפני טורח צבור מפני התענית וי"א שמתפללים י"ח שלימות מפני שצ"ל הבדלה בחונן הדעת ותימה אמאי לא פריך ונכללה בהביננו וי"ל דלא דמי דהתם כל השנה כולה מתפלל י"ח ואין לנו להקשות ונכללה מכלל כדי לשנות המנהג של כל השנה אבל הכא שכל השנה מתפלל הביננו פריך שפיר למה לי לשנות המנהג בשביל אתה חוננתנו ונכללה בהביננו.

Tosafot, Berachot 29a

Let one include it in Havineinu – That which the Talmud says in the first chapter of Niddah (8b), throughout the year one recites *Shemoneh Esreh*, except at the conclusion of Yom Kippur, because of the burden it places upon the congregation due to the fast; some say that one must still recite the full eighteen blessings because one needs to say *Havdalah* in the blessing of *Chonein HaDa'at* (Who grants wisdom). Query: Why did the Talmud not [simply] ask, include it in *Havineinu*? One may answer that the case [in Niddah] is not comparable [i.e., it begins with a different premise], in that throughout the year one recites *Shemoneh Esreh*, therefore it is not appropriate for us to ask about including [*Havdalah*] amongst them [in *Havineinu*], which would deviate from the year-round practice. However here [in Berachot], where [the discussion is predicated on the fact that] throughout the year one recites *Havineinu*, it is appropriate to ask, why should we deviate from the year-round practice because of *Atah Chonantanu* – [simply] include [*Havdalah*] in *Havineinu*.

Tosafot note that whereas in Berachot 29a, Mar Zutra proposes including *Havdalah* in *Havineinu*, no similar suggestion is put forth in the passage in Niddah. Tosafot explain that the discussion in Niddah 8a is based on a different premise than that of Berachot 29a. In Berachot 29a, it is assumed that *Havineinu* is familiar to the community, while in the situation being discussed in Niddah 8a, the community generally does *not* recite *Havineinu*. In situations where *Havineinu* is the standard practice (i.e., Berachot 29a), suggestions are made to attempt to uphold the norm. But when the situation is such that reciting *Havineinu* would itself be a deviation from the norm (Niddah 8a), no such ideas are proposed.

Tosafot's commentary draws a distinction between the two Gemarot based upon regular practice and deviations from it. The Gemara's objective is to avoid mistakes in prayer, and an essential factor leading to mistakes is one's familiarity—or lack thereof. If a community is accustomed to reciting a prayer often, then its members generally have a high level of familiarity with it. At the same time, the Gemara is attempting to uphold the practice of communities who regularly recite *Havineinu*. Thus, in cases such as the Gemara in Berachot 29a, where a community's regular practice is to recite *Havineinu*, and who are therefore presumed to have a familiarity with *Havineinu*, suggestions to facilitate the continuation of this practice are called for, including modifications for the conclusion of Shabbat and festivals or for the rainy season. Conversely, for communities where this is not the case, it becomes less essential to look for ways to allow for the recitation of *Havineinu*.

A change in reading: the elimination of encumbrance

Although the explanations of most commentaries presented thus far limit the recitation of *Havineinu*, other commentators follow Mar Zutra's suggestions—thus allowing *Havineinu* within a broader collection of situations. Rashba allows for *Havineinu* at the conclusion of Shabbat and festivals. Tosafot's novel approach suggests that the case being discussed on Berachot 29a is that of a community which regularly recites *Havineinu*, and therefore there is merit in attempting to maintain the community practice. A direct result of this regularity in practice is increased fluency and proficiency in prayer. Rabbeinu Manoach considers the concern of encumbrance (as defined by Beit Yosef and Bach) to be eliminated due to this familiarity.

Rabbeinu Manoach rules that one who is familiar and somewhat proficient with the text can recite *Havineinu* with Mar Zutra's modifications. His ruling is cited in several thirteenth century works from Provence and later gains wider notice. Kessef Mishneh is one source which cites this ruling:

כסף משנה הלכות תפילה ונשיאת כפים פרק ב הלכה ד

...וכתב ה"ר מנוח דבגמרא פריך בין אימות הגשמים בין אמו"ש וי"ט ונכלליה מכלל ומשני דילמא אתי לאיטרודי משמע שאם מובטח דלא אתי לאיטרודי רשאי כדאמרינן גבי נשיאות כפים עכ"ל

Kessef Mishneh, Laws of Prayer 2:4
...Rabbeinu Manoach wrote that the Talmud challenged, in both the cases of the rainy season and the conclusion of Shabbat and festivals: [Mar Zutra's proposition, namely] let one include [*Havdalah*] amongst them [in *Havineinu*], and it answered that one may come to be encumbered. This implies that if one is certain that one will not come to be encumbered, one is permitted [to say *Havineinu* in these circumstances], as is the rule regarding the Priestly Blessing.

Rabbeinu Manoach assumes that the Gemara has no difficulties with Mar Zutra's inclusions aside from the possibility that one may become encumbered. He subscribes to the simplest reading of the text, not considering other problems such as Rabbeinu Yonah's theory as to the barrier to adding *Havdalah*. Accordingly, people who are familiar enough with the prayer to preclude encumbrance or confusion may add supplements into *Havineinu*. Kessef Mishnah refers to a case of a *chazzan* (congregational prayer leader) who also wants to participate in *birkat kohanim* (the Priestly Blessing) as a proof.

The parallel case of Birkat Kohanim *(the Priestly Blessing)*

When a Kohen is leading services and still wishes to be involved in reciting the priestly blessing, a strong potential for confusion exists, because after reciting the priestly blessing he may make a mistake in his duties of leading services. Because of this potential confusion, he is not allowed to perform both functions. But when he is confident of his ability to perform both roles without confusion or error, he may act as prayer leader and offer the priestly blessing. Rabbeinu Manoach applies this reasoning to the question of additions to *Havineinu*—he endorses *Havineinu* with additions as long as the likelihood of error or confusion is slim.

Shulchan Aruch codifies the ruling of a Kohen who is free from potential error:

שולחן ערוך, אורח חיים קכח:כ

אם ש"צ כהן, אם יש שם כהנים אחרים, לא ישא את כפיו; (ולא יאמרו לו לעלות או ליטול ידיו, אבל אם אמרו לו צריך לעלות, דהוא עובר בעשה אם אינו עולה) (מרדכי פרק הקורא עומד והגהות מיימוני פרק ט"ו דתפלה ואגור). ואפי' אין שם כהן אלא הוא, לא ישא את כפיו אא"כ מובטח לו שיחזור לתפלתו בלא טירוף דעת, שאם הוא מובטח בכך כיון שאין שם כהן אלא הוא ישא את כפיו כדי שלא תתבטל נשיאות כפים.

Shulchan Aruch, Orach Chaim 128:20
If the leader of the prayers is a Kohen and if there are other Kohanim present, the leader should not offer the Priestly Blessing. Even if he is the only Kohen, he should not offer the Priestly Blessing, unless he is certain that he will be able to return to his prayers without his mind becoming confused. If he is certain of this, since there is no other Kohen there, one should offer the Priestly Blessing so that it not be neglected.

Here, Shulchan Aruch clearly specifies that becoming confused is the primary problem confronting a Kohen who is both leading prayers and wants to participate in the Priestly Blessing.

When examining this ruling, Magen Avraham considers the new reality that has developed in his day: the widespread use of printed texts. He argues that praying from a text (as opposed to from memory) prevents confusion when the Kohen concludes the Priestly Blessing and returns to the *Shemoneh Esreh*. Therefore, if one is using a *siddur*, he is free to perform both his duties as *chazzan* and Kohen, since there is no concern that he will err.

מגן אברהם סימן קכח ס"ק לא
מובטח שיחזור - ולדידן שמתפללין מתוך הסידור מובטח שיחזור לתפלתו

ומ"מ כשיש כהנים אחרים לא יעקור רגליו [ל"ח]... ובנ"ץ כתוב שסומכין על שמתפללין מתוך הסידור... לכן נ"ל דבמקום שאין מנהג לא ישא כפיו אם יש כהנים אחרים וכדעת כל הגאונים...

Magen Avraham, Orach Chaim 128:31

Certain that he will be able to return – and for us, who pray from a printed text, we are always certain that the leader will be able to return to his prayers [without becoming confused]. Nevertheless, when there are other Kohanim present [i.e., another viable option besides relying on the printed text] one should not move one's feet [to prepare to offer the Blessing] (source: Lechem Chamudot). [Magen Avraham continues to discuss other approaches to this issue.] The Nachalat Tzvi wrote that [the current practice] relies on the fact that we now pray from printed texts. [Magen Avraham continues by disputing the legitimacy of this claim on various grounds, but he concludes that] it appears to me that wherever there is no set custom, the leader should not offer the Priestly Blessing if other Kohanim are present, in accordance with all the great decisors...

When an alternative solution is available, it is not preferable for a Kohen to both lead the congregation in prayer and offer the Priestly Blessing. But when such a resolution does not exist, Magen Avraham recognizes that a change in technology—the printed prayer book—could be a factor that would allow a Kohen to perform both services. With the proliferation of prayer books, there is much less concern of confusion or accidental error. Thus, when there is no potential for error, it is permissible to recite *Havineinu*.

This position is clearly cited by Meiri in the name of "one of the great commentators," generally thought to be Ravad:[11]

המאירי בית הבחירה ברכות כח עמוד ב–ל עמוד א

אם בטוח בעצמו שלא לטעות והוא שעת הדחק מותר על דעת גדולי המפרשים.

Meiri, Beit HaBechirah Commentary to Berachot 28b–30a

If one is certain of oneself that one will not err, and it is a time of

---

[11] Although no extant text authored by Ravad states this, Sefer HaMichtam by Rabbi David ben Levi of Narbonne quotes Ravad as saying such; see citation in HaTzava KaHalacha, below p. 113.

pressing need, one is permitted [to say a condensed version of *Shemoneh Esreh*] by the opinion of one of the great commentators (Ravad).

Developing previous opinions, Rabbeinu Manoach (and Ravad) ruled in accordance with Mar Zutra's inclusions. There are many arguments for and against this ruling, all explained in previous sections. Magen Avraham's reasoning—that a prayer book reduces confusion in prayer—continues in a similar vein. While both Rabbeinu Manoach's logical approach to the Gemara and Magen Avraham's incorporation of technological advancements are valid reasons for ruling in accordance with Mar Zutra's inclusions, the Talmud Yerushalmi is an explicit support. Strangely, however, this supporting source is missing from most commentaries.

The Yerushalmi: a different text of Havineinu *with additions*

Various commentators allow *Havineinu* to be recited, even during the rainy season or at conclusion of Shabbat and festivals, provided that one is certain that the additions will not cause confusion. The permissibility of this practice, and its justification, are discussed at length. Startlingly, though, most commentators fail to cite an obvious, strong proof for this approach—a Talmudic passage (parallel to Berachot 29a) in Yerushalmi Berachot. The Yerushalmi's version of the text of *Havineinu* includes an explicit addition for the rainy season:

תלמוד ירושלמי מסכת ברכות פרק ד ה"ג \ דף ח טור א
אי זו היא שבע מעין שמנה עשר רב אמר סוף כל ברכה וברכה ושמואל
אמ' ראש כל ברכה וברכה אית תניי תני שבע מעין שמונה עשרה ואית
תניי תני שמונה עשרה מעין שמונה עשרה מאן דמר שבע מעין שמונה
עשרה מסייע לשמואל ומאן דמר י"ח מעין י"ח מסייעא לרב רבי זעורא
שלח לר' נחום גבי רבי יניי ביר' ישמעאל אמ' ליה אי זו היא מעין שבע
מעין שמונה עשרה דשמואל אמר ליה הביניינו רצה תשובתינו סלח לנו
גואלינו רפא חלייינו ברך שנותינו אמר רבי חגיי אם היו גשמים אומרים
בגשמי ברכה אם היו טללים אומ' בטללי ברכה [וכו']

Talmud Yerushalmi, Berachot 4:3 (8a)

What is the seven-fold abstraction of eighteen? Rav said: The conclusion of each blessing. Shmuel said: The beginning of each blessing. Some taught: a seven-fold abstraction of eighteen; some taught: an eighteen-fold abstraction of eighteen. The one who says "a seven-fold abstraction of eighteen" supports the view of Shmuel; the one who says "an eighteen-fold abstraction of eighteen" supports the view of Rav. Rabbi Zeora sent a question to Rav Nachum via Rabbi Yannai son of Rabbi Yishmael. He asked: What is Shmuel's seven-fold abstraction of eighteen? He replied: "Grant us wisdom (*Havineinu*), accept our repentance, forgive us our redeemer, heal our sick, bless our years..." — Rabbi Chaggai said: In the rainy season one says [the additional insertion of] "with rains of blessing"; in the summer season one says "with dews of blessing"... [The Talmud continues with the rest of the *Havineinu* text according to the Yerushalmi.]

The Yerushalmi appears to clarify the seeming difficulties in the Bavli's presentation. The Bavli presents two passages which seem to limit the utility of *Havineinu* due to required additions which cannot be made; each is challenged by Mar Zutra, asking why not simply include the required addition in *Havineinu*. For one proposal, the passage is left with a question—*kushya*; for the other, the Talmud offers an explicit rebuttal. The Yerushalmi, by contrast, states explicitly: one *may* add to *Havineinu* an appropriate request for rain—the addition seemingly rejected by the Bavli! Surprisingly, though, the Yerushalmi remains unacknowledged by the majority of commentators, especially those who would benefit from bringing it to support their positions.

Puzzlingly, very few authorities cite the Yerushalmi—even when discussing Rabbeinu Manoach's position. Kessef Mishneh writes:

כסף משנה הלכות תפילה ונשיאת כפים פרק ב הלכה ד
ובקשתי לו חבר ולא מצאתי

Kessef Mishneh, Laws of Prayer 2:4
I have searched for a supporting opinion but did not found one.

Kessef Mishneh's words seem to imply that he is completely unaware of the Yerushalmi passage. In fact, few commentators seem to acknowledge the existence of this text at all. Among the exceptions are Rashi in his Siddur, Kol Bo, and Meiri.

Rashi includes the text of the Yerushalmi into his Siddur:

סידור רש"י סימן נח

...אומר שלש ברכות ראשונות, ואחר כך אומר הביננו [ה' אלהינו] רצה
בתשובתינו סלח לנו גואלינו רפא חליינו וברך שנותינו, ואמר ר' חגי אם
היו [ימות] גשמים [אומר] בגשמי (נדבה) [ברכה,], ואם היו טללים
[אומר] בטללי ברכה...

Siddur Rashi 58

...One should recite the first three blessings, and afterwards say
"Grant us wisdom (*Havineinu*) [Lord our God], accept our
repentance, forgive us our redeemer, heal our sick, bless our
years [with sustinance]..." And Rabbi Chaggai said: in the rainy
season, one says [the additional insertion of] "with rains of
blessing"; in the dewy [summer] season, [one says] "with dews
of blessing" ...

Additionally, Kol Bo notes:

ספר כלבו סימן יא ד"ה כל הברכות

ובירושלמי נמצא נוסח אחר בברכה הזאת, הביננו ה' אלהינו ורצה
תשובתינו סלח לנו גואלינו ורפא חליינו ברך שנותינו בטללי ברכה ובימות
הגשמים אומר בגשמי ברכה כי מפוזרים אתה תקבץ ותועי עליך לשפוט
ועל הרשעים תשת ידך וישמחו כל חוסים בך בבנין עירך ובחידוש בית
מקדשך טרם נקרא ואתה תענה וכו' כאמור כמו בנוסח האחר, נראה לפי
הירושלמי שמתפללין אותה אפילו בימות הגשמים, ויש אומרים
שבמוצאי שבתות וימים טובים שצריך לומר הבדלה בחונן הדעת ובימות
הגשמים שצריך לומר שאלה בברכת השנים אין מתפללין תפלה זו.

Kol Bo Ch. 11, s.v. *kol ha-berachot*

A different version of this blessing can be found in the
Yerushalmi: "Grant us wisdom, Lord our God, and accept our
repentance, forgive us our redeemer, heal our sick, bless our
years with dew of blessing"—and during the rainy season one
says, "with rains of blessing"—"for You gather the scattered,
judge those who stray, and punish the wicked with Your hand;
may those who trust in You rejoice over the building of Your city
and the restoration of Your temple. For You answer us before we
call, etc.," as the other version. According to the Yerushalmi, it
seems that one should recite [*Havineinu*] even during the rainy
season. Some say that after Shabbat and festivals, when one must
say *Havdalah* in *Chonein HaDa'at*, and during the rainy season,
when one must ask [for rain] in *Birkat HaShanim*, one should not
recite this prayer.

The Kol Bo seems to emphasize the Yerushalmi's version of the blessing. He only cites the other, widely accepted view as "Some say," implying that he himself subscribes to the opinion of the Yerushalmi, like Rashi above does.

Meiri is also aware of authorities who rule in accordance with the Yerushalmi. After discussing the view of Ravad and other Spanish authorities who rule that *Havineinu* may be said at the conclusion of Shabbat and festivals but not during the rainy season, he notes:

המאירי בית הבחירה ברכות כח עמוד ב–ל עמוד א
ובחבורי קצת רבני צרפת ראיתי שכוללים בה שאלה בשם תלמוד המערב
וברך שנותינו בגשמי ברכה.
Meiri, Beit HaBechirah Commentary to Berachot 28b–30a
In the compositions of some French authorities I have seen that they include the request for rain [in *Havineinu*] in the name of the Western (i.e., Jerusalem) Talmud: "bless our years with rains of blessing."

While some French authorities (perhaps Siddur Rashi) are inclined to rule in accordance with the Yerushalmi, Meiri himself includes such views in his commentary but seems less inclined than his contemporary Kol Bo to endorse such a view (perhaps because as he collects a wide variety of sources from Spain, Italy, Egypt, and North Africa, in addition to France and Provence, he sees hardly any others who do so). By the period of codification, these few commentators carry little weight with later authorities.

Aruch HaShulchan is one of the few later authorities who does mention the Yerushalmi:

ערוך השולחן אורח חיים סימן קי:ד
...ותדע שיש מחלוקת בסברא דטרודי שהרי בירושלמי שם אומר באמת
על ימות הגשמים שיכללנה ע"ש
Aruch HaShulchan, Orach Chaim 110:4
...Know that there is a dispute regarding the rationale of encumbrance, for in the Yerushalmi there, it says that indeed during the rainy season one may include [the request for rain in *Havineinu*] – see there.

One might argue that the omission of the Yerushalmi in most sources stems from its lack of relevance or authority or both. But this is certainly not the case: the Yerushalmi's version of *Havineinu*, parallel to the passage in the Bavli, is certainly relevant, as it would be an excellent—indeed, decisive—support for Mar Zutra. Moreover, the Yerushalmi traditionally carries a great deal of weight in halachic discussions. Specifically, some authorities employ the principle that a dispute in the Bavli is ruled according to whichever opinion is brought alone in the Yerushalmi (when such is the case). The question of *Havineinu* certainly seems to fit this criterion!

3.2 The limited utility of *Havineinu* versus situations of *dechak*

As we have seen, many authorities limit the times that one is permitted to recite *Havineinu* to approximately half the year. One may not recite *Havineinu* at the conclusions of Shabbat and festivals or during the rainy season. But this standard ruling does not address the very situation that compels one to recite *Havineinu*: *sha'at ha-dechak*. In such circumstances, options for prayer are limited. Time constraints and outside pressures could preclude a full *Shemoneh Esreh*, and the only feasible alternatives would be *Havineinu* or no prayer at all.

Rambam, Tur, and Shulchan Aruch prohibit *Havineinu* both at the conclusion of Shabbat and festivals, and during the rainy season. Yet they also state in their codes that *Havineinu* is recited in emergencies, when it is not possible to recite the full text. Although these authorities' rulings proscribe the recitation of *Havineinu* during certain times of the year, other authorities consider the possibility that there might be room to allow a person in extenuating circumstances to recite *Havineinu* even at those times.

What basis might there be for exceptions to the ruling that insertions may not be made into *Havineinu*? Rabbi Akiva Eiger distinguishes between two types of *dechak*—a lesser level, which authorizes one to recite *Havineinu* generally, and a more extreme one, which can even exempt one from the rule prohibiting the use of *Havineinu* at the conclusion of Shabbat and festivals and during the rainy season. If the chance of interruption exists, although this qualifies as *sha'at ha-dechak*, it does not override the rule concerning additions into *Havineinu*, and one must recite the full *Shemoneh Esreh*.

הגהות רבי עקיבא איגר אורח חיים קי:א

ולא במוצאי שבת ויום טוב- אפשר דקאי על שעת הדחק דמחבר, דהיינו שירא שיפסיקוהו עוברי דרכים, בזה במוצאי שבת ויום טוב אף דהבדלה אינו מעכב דהרי לא הבדיל בתפלה אינו חוזר ומתפלל, (ו)מכל מקום טוב יותר להתפלל בדרך ובנוסחא הראויה, ואם יפסיקוהו יפסיקוהו, ויגמור אח"כ התפלה. אבל בדחק שמזכיר המג"א בריש הסימן או השעה עוברת, י"ל דבזה במוצאי שבת ויום טוב מוטב שיתפלל הביננו ולא יזכיר הבדלה, ממה שלא יתפלל כלל. ובימות הגשמים י"ל דבלא הזכיר משיב הרוח אינו תפלה כלל, אבל במוצאי שבת ויום טוב בלא הבדלה דיוצא ידי התפלה, י"ל דעדיף יותר ממה שלא (התפלל) [יתפלל] כלל, וצ"ע לדינא:

R Akiva Eiger, Notes to Orach Chaim 110:1

Nor at the conclusion of Shabbat or festivals – perhaps this is referring to the first instance of *sha'at ha-dechak* mentioned by the author [of the Shulchan Aruch], namely that one is afraid one will be interrupted by passersby: in that case, at the conclusion of Shabbat or festivals—even though *Havdalah* does not prevent one from fulfilling their obligation of prayer, for if one did not insert *Havdalah* into one's prayers, one does not repeat the *Shemoneh Esreh*—nonetheless, it is better to pray while traveling and with the appropriate text (i.e., the full *Shemoneh Esreh*), and if one gets interrupted, one gets interrupted, and one then completes one's prayer afterward. However, in the case of *dechak* mentioned by the Magen Avraham at the beginning of §110, or when the time for prayer is about to run out [so that one is faced with a choice of *Havineinu* or nothing], one might say that in this instance, at the conclusion of Shabbat or festivals it is better to recite *Havineinu* and not mention *Havdalah* than not to pray at all. With regard to prayer during the rainy season, one might say that without the insertion for rain, one has not prayed at all; however, at the conclusion of Shabbat or festivals, when without *Havdalah* one has still fulfilled one's obligation of prayer, one might say that this is preferable to not praying at all. This analysis requires further investigation before ruling accordingly.

Essentially, Rabbi Akiva Eiger takes into account two types of variables—the level of *dechak*, and the type of insertion that is required. He is willing to allow for the recitation of *Havineinu* only when the level of *dechak* is high and the only insertion required is *Havdalah*. In all other circumstances, such as during the rainy season or in lesser levels of *dechak*, he prohibits the use of *Havineinu*. (See Table 3.7.)

Rabbi Akiva Eiger's reasoning is as follows: At times when no insertions are required, one may certainly recite *Havineinu* when in a situation of *dechak*. At times when special insertions are required, such as the conclusion of Shabbat and festivals and during the rainy season, one generally may not recite *Havineinu*. Rabbi Akiva Eiger suggests one exception to this rule. While one may never recite *Havineinu* when required to insert *she'elat geshamim*, one may be able to recite *Havineinu* at the conclusion of Shabbat and festivals under certain circumstances. To understand this difference, one must note that although it is preferable to recite *Havdalah* both during prayer and again in the *Havdalah* ceremony, if *Havdalah* is omitted during prayer, one may fulfill one's obligation to mark the conclusion of Shabbat solely through the *Havdalah* ceremony.[12] While not ideal, Rabbi Akiva Eiger allows one to forego *Havdalah* during prayer in an extreme case of *dechak*—when one is running out of time. Whereas lesser forms of *dechak* might only affect prayer through interruption or causing a lower level of concentration, running out of time threatens one's very ability to pray at all. Given that prospect, Rabbi Akiva Eiger suggests that *Havineinu*—even without an insertion for *Havdalah*— might be a suitable alternative.

If one is able to fulfill one's obligation to mark the conclusion of Shabbat independently of adding a paragraph of *Havdalah* to *Shemoneh Esreh,* why do we limit Rabbi Akiva Eiger's leniency to a case of a more imposing *dechak*, namely time running out? Why is it that in a regular situation of *sha'at ha-dechak* one cannot simply recite *Havineinu* without any additions, and say *Havdalah* afterward over a cup of wine? Immediately following the

---

[12] Shulchan Aruch, Orach Chaim 294:1.

Table 3.7
The permissibility of reciting *Havineinu* in different situations – the view of Rabbi Akiva Eiger

	Regular day (no insertion)	Conclusion of Shabbat and festivals (*Havdalah* insertion)	Rainy Season (*She'elat geshamim* insertion)
No *dechak*	NO	NO	NO
Mild *dechak* (fear of interruptions)	YES	NO	NO
Extreme *dechak* (e.g., running out of time)	YES	YES	NO

discussion which disallows *Havineinu* at the conclusion of Shabbat and festivals and during the rainy season, the Gemara addresses this specific question:

תלמוד בבלי מסכת ברכות דף כט עמוד א

והבדלה בחונן הדעת - אין מחזירין אותו, מפני שיכול לאומרה על הכוס! - טעה שאני.

Babylonian Talmud, Berachot 29a
[One who erred and did not mention] *Havdalah* in the blessing of *Chonein HaDa'at*, we do not make him return to the beginning, for one may say it later on a cup of wine [in the *Havdalah* ceremony]? Error is [a] different [case].

It is true that *ex post facto (be-de'avad)*, were one to recite *Shemoneh Esreh* without *Havdalah*, one would nonetheless fulfill one's obligation to pray. But one may not choose *ab initio (lechatchilah)* to omit *Havdalah* in prayer, as only accidents are allotted this special dispensation. Surprisingly, Rabbi Akiva Eiger proposes a *preemptive* decision that seems not to be *ex post facto*. How can one dispense with one's obligation to recite *Havdalah*? Bi'ur Halacha provides an answer. There is a general principle in halacha that *sha'at ha-dechak* is equivalent to an *ex post facto* situation. Therefore, under such extreme pressure, one may preemptively decide to recite *Havineinu*, aware that this would involve skipping *Havdalah*, since this action could be considered similar to the case of accidental error.

ביאור הלכה סימן קי

ואינו מתפלל הביננו וכו' - ולא במו"ש ויו"ט. עיין בחידושי רע"א שמסתפק לענין מו"ש ויו"ט אם השעה עוברת י"ל דבזה במו"ש ויו"ט מוטב שיתפלל הביננו ולא יזכיר הבדלה דעכ"פ בדיעבד יצא בעלמא בלא הבדלה ממה שלא יתפלל כלל עי"ש עוד:

Bi'ur Halacha, Orach Chaim 110

One does not recite Havineinu... nor at the conclusion of Shabbat or festivals – See the Novellae of Rabbi Akiva Eiger where he is unsure of this rule with regard to the conclusion of Shabbat and festivals if time is running out, for one might argue that at the conclusion of Shabbat and festivals it would be better to recite *Havineinu* and not mention *Havdalah*, so one will at least [imperfectly] fulfills one's obligation [of prayer] without *Havdalah*, rather than not pray at all. See there for more.

Until now, only in *ex post facto* cases of error would one be able to omit *Havdalah* at the end of Shabbat and festivals. Rabbi Akiva Eiger, however, introduces a dispensation for one who may be unable to pray altogether. Bi'ur Halacha explains that this ruling is not novel. One must simply understand that such a preemptive decision should also be considered *ex post facto* despite its omission prior to the time of prayer. This exception, though, does not extend to *she'elat geshamim*, which does not have an alternative means of fulfillment, and thus, if omitted, one must repeat the entire *Shemoneh Esreh*. (See Table 3.8.)

Rabbi Akiva Eiger discusses an extreme case of *dechak*: when the time period for prayer is about to end and one may miss an opportunity to pray altogether if one does not recite *Havineinu*. Such a situation leaves an individual with a choice between reciting *Havineinu* and not praying at all. Chayei Adam describes a similar case of an ill individual who finds it difficult to pray:

Table 3.8
Comparison of additions for *Havdalah* and for rain

Addition	Where Added into *Shemoneh Esreh*	What to do if forgotten	Does it make a practical difference if a misconception develops?	If omitted, has one fulfilled one's obligation?
Havdalah	*Atah Chonantanu*	Do not repeat *Shemoneh Esreh*	Yes	Yes
She'elat geshamim (Rain supplication)	*Birkat HaShanim*	Repeat *Shemoneh Esreh*	No	No

חיי אדם כלל כד הלכות תפלה סעיף לא

בשעת הדחק כגון שהוא בדרך במקום שירא שיפסיקוהו עוברי דרכים או
שירא שיעבור זמן תפלה או חולה, מתפלל ג' ראשונות ואח"כ אומר מעין
י"ח והיינו שאומר נוסח זה, הבינינו ה' אלהינו ... אבל במוצ"ש ויו"ט
שצריך לומר הבדלה וכן בימות הגשמים שצריך לומר טל ומטר, אין
מתפללין הבינינו (ק"י). ומ"מ בחולה או שעת הדחק גדול, יכול להתפלל
אף בימות הגשמים או במוצ"ש ולקצר בכל ברכה כדלקמן כלל כ"ה סי'
א"ב...

Chayei Adam, Laws of Prayer 24:31

In a time of pressing need—e.g., one is traveling in a place where
one is afraid one will be interrupted by passers-by, or one is
afraid that the time for prayer will pass, or one is ill—one recites
the first three blessings and then says an abstraction of *Shemoneh
Esreh*, namely the following text: Grant us, Lord, our God
(*Havineinu*)... However, at the conclusion of Shabbat and
festivals, when one must say *Havdalah*, and similarly during the
rainy season when one must add '[and give] dew and rain,' one
may not recite *Havineinu* (Orach Chaim 110). Nonetheless, one
who is ill, or in case of great pressing need (*sha'at ha-dechak*), may
recite [a similar short prayer] even during the rainy season or at
the conclusion of Shabbat and condense each blessing, as was
written below, §25, para. 1–2.

Here, Chayei Adam lists illness along with other examples of pressing need, thereby equating ill health with *sha'at ha-dechak*. Consequently, one who is ill may recite *Havineinu*, even at the conclusion of Shabbat and festivals or during the rainy season. Notably, this position introduces illness as a further example of *sha'at ha-dechak*, as mentioned previously in Chapter One. Chayei Adam could very well be understood as saying that one may recite *Havineinu* in any situation of *sha'at ha-dechak*.

Instead of formulating the exception for the sick based on *sha'at ha-dechak*, another option would be to apply the leniency suggested by Rabbeinu Manoach and Ravad—that if one is confident that one will not err, one may recite *Havineinu* even after Shabbat and festivals and during the rainy season:[13]

גשר החיים א:ג)(ה)

והנראה שאפי' לדעת איזה אחרונים האומרים שהאידנא לא נהיגין בתפלת הבינינו (ראה כף החיים ק"י) מסתבר שבחולה שאני. כן גם נראה שאף אמנם נקטי' שאין תפלת הבינינו בחורף, שצריכין להזכיר ותן טו"ל ולא במוצש"ק ובמוציו"ט שצריכין לומר אתה חוננתנו–הנה בחולה אפשר לסמוך על הפוסקים שבאם יודע שיזכור לומר ותן טו"מ בחורף ולומר המבדיל בין קודש לחול במוצ"ש אפשר להקל לחולה גם בימות הגשמים ובמוצ"ש.

Gesher HaChaim §1:3(5)

It seems that even according to those latter-day authorities who say that nowadays our custom is not to recite *Havineinu* (see Kaf HaChaim 110), it would seem logical that illness is different. So too it would appear that even though the classical sources rule that one may not recite *Havineinu* during the winter, for one must add the additional prayer for rain, nor at the conclusion of Shabbat and festivals, for one must say *Atah Chonantanu* (*Havdalah*)—a sick person may rely on those decisors who rule that one may say *Havineinu* if one is certain that one will remember to add the additional prayer for rain during the winter, or to say the statement of *Havdalah* at the conclusion of Shabbat; [therefore,] one may be lenient for a sick individual even during the rainy season or at the conclusion of Shabbat.

---

[13] Above, page 97.

The Gesher HaChaim builds upon the precedent of Rabbeinu Manoach, Ravad, and others. The reason one may not recite *Havineinu* during times of year when special insertions are to be made is that one may err in one's prayer. However, if one is certain that one will not err, Rabbeinu Manoach and Ravad see no reason to prohibit reciting *Havineinu*. Thus, this conceptual leniency based on one's level of proficiency leads Gesher HaChaim to make an exception for an ill person in similar circumstances.

A further expansion of the view of Rabbeinu Manoach and Ravad arises from a situation unique to our own time. HaTzava KaHalacha, a handbook for Israeli soldiers by R. Yitzchak Kofman, applies the rulings of previous authorities to conditions in contemporary Israel. Building on the examples of *dechak* presented by Rabbi Akiva Eiger, Chayei Adam, and Gesher HaChaim, HaTzava KaHalacha again expands the applicability of *Havineinu*. Similar to the cases above, soliders have rigorous and ever-changing schedules that include many unforeseen and unplanned events. Military service also generates innumerable situations which could be included as *dechak*. Additionally, HaTzava KaHalacha adopts the reasoning of Rabbeinu Manoach and Ravad to permit *Havineinu* on the basis that a prayer book prevents confusion. Rabbi Kofman even cites the contrary view of the Bi'ur Halacha in a footnote in order to refute it.

הצבא כהלכה פרק מג

בשעת דחק גדולה, אפשר להתפלל "שמונה עשרה" בנוסח "ברכת הבינינו" (כגון שהוא בדרך, או שהיה עומד במקום שהוא טרוד וירא שיפסיקוהו, או שלא יוכל להתפלל בכוונה תפילה ארוכה), גם בימות הגשמים ומוצאי שבת[26]. אופן התפילה: מתפלל 3 ברכות ראשונות של "שמונה עשרה", "תפילת הבינינו", ו-3 ברכות אחרונות. אין צריך באמירת "אלוקי נצור". אך יאמר הפסוק: "יהיו לרצון" וגו', ויפסע 3 פסיעות עם אמירת "עושה שלום" וגו'. בימים שאומרים "הלל" ו"מוסף"–יש צורך להוסיפם.

26. אף שב"ביאור הלכה" (ד"ה "או") כתב שהיום אין נוהגים להתפלל "הבינינו". אין הדבר מוסכם ופסוק, ומשאר פוסקים לא משמע הכי. בשו"ע (שם) מבואר, שבימות הגשמים שצריך לומר טל ומטר וכן במוצאי שבת ויום טוב, אין מתפללים "הבינינו" ומקורו ממסכת ברכות

(דף כ"ט עמוד א), וכן נכתב בדיני תפילה לחייל (בפרק תפילה קצרה לחיילים, סעיף ג). אולם, לדעתי אפשר לעת הצורך להקל ולהסתמך על הדעות שגם בימות הגשמים ומוצאי שבת ויו"ט אפשר להתפלל "הבינו", באופן שיכלול בקשת הגשם או ההבדלה, בהסתמך על רבינו מנוח שהובא ב"כסף משנה" (הלכות תפילה פרק ב, הלכה ד) והוזכר ב"מגן אברהם" (סימן ק"י ס"ק ד), וכן כתב רבינו מנוח בפירוש (בספר המנוחה עמוד ס"א), וכן היא דעת "המאורות" ו"המכתם" בשם הראב"ד, שהטעם שנאמר בגמרא: "דילמא אתי לאטרודי", אינו שייך אם בטוח שלא יטעה ויוכל להזכיר הנ"ל ולחזור למקומו, וכן הוא מנהג תימן כמודפס בסידור תכלאל (עץ חיים חלק א עמוד צ"ד) בתוספת המלים: "בימות הגשמים ותן טל ומטר" לאחר המילים: "ושכננו בנאות ארצך". שם, בביאור עץ חיים, כתב: "ונ"ל דאם יש סידור לפניו שאומר מתוכו, ליכא מאן דפליג דלא אתי לאטרודי". וכן כולל ההבדלה "הבינו" המבדיל בין קודש לחול לדעת דרכיך" וגו', (אף שלגבי ההבדלה בכלל לא נאמר הטעם של איטרודי). הגם ששיטה זו אינה מוסכמת על הכל, מ"מ כדאים הם רבינו מנוח, "המכתם" בשם הראב"ד, ו"המאורות", לסמוך עליהם בשעת הדחק.—כל הנ"ל על פי הגר"ש דבליצקי שליט"א. שוב ראיתי, שבדומה כתב ב"גשר החיים" (סימן ג) ביחס לחולה.

HaTzava KaHalacha Ch. 43

In cases of great pressing need, one may recite "*Shemoneh Esreh*" with the text of *Havineinu* (for example, if one is traveling, or one is standing in a place where one is encumbered and afraid of being interrupted, or one is unable to direct one's intention for a full-length prayer), even during the rainy season or at the conclusion of Shabbat.[26] The manner of this prayer is as follows: One recites the first three blessings of *Shemoneh Esreh*, then the *Havineinu* prayer, then the final three blessings. One need not say the additional paragraph "My God, guard my tongue"; however, one should say the verse, "Let the words of my mouth be acceptable..." (Ps. 19:15). One then steps three steps backward while saying the line, "The One who makes peace on high..." On days when Hallel or Mussaf is said—one must add them.

26. Even though Bi'ur Halacha (Orach Chaim 110, s.v. *oh*) wrote that nowadays the practice is not to say *Havineinu*, the matter is not universally agreed to or set, and the other decisors do not seem to imply this. In Shulchan Aruch (ibid.) it is explained that during the rainy season, when one must insert an additional prayer for rain, and similarly at the conclusion of Shabbat and festivals, one may not recite *Havineinu*, and the source of this rule is in tractate Berachot (29a), and so was written in *Laws of*

Prayer for a Soldier (Chapter *The Short Prayer for Soldiers*, para. 3). However, in my opinion, it is possible to be lenient in times of need and rely on the views that even during the rainy season and at the conclusion of Shabbat and festivals one may recite *Havineinu* in a manner that includes an additional prayer for rain or *Havdalah*, relying on the view of Rabbeinu Manoach which is cited in Kessef Mishneh (Laws of Prayer 2:4) and mentioned in Magen Avraham (Orach Chaim 110:4), and which Rabbeinu Manoach wrote explicitly (Sefer HaMenuchah, p. 61), and such is the also the view of the Meorot, and the Michtam in the name of the Ravad, that the reason given in the Talmud, "that one may come to be encumbered," does not apply if one is certain that one will not err—thus one can make the required additions and return to one's place. Such is the custom of the Yemenite community, as published in Siddur Tachlael (Etz Chaim vol. 1, p. 94) with the addition of the words: "During the rainy season [insert the words] 'send dew and rain' after the words, 'bring us to dwell in your bountiful land.'" In the Etz Chaim commentary there, it explains: "It seems to me that if one has a prayer book set out before oneself from which one reads, no one would disagree that such a person would not come to be encumbered." [That *siddur*] also includes the *Havdalah*: "Grant us, Lord, our God, the One who distinguishes between holy and profane, wisdom to understand your ways, etc." (even though regarding *Havdalah*, the rationale of becoming encumbered is not explicitly mentioned). Despite the fact that this view is not universally agreed to, nonetheless Rabbeinu Manoach, the Michtam in the name of the Ravad, and the Meorot are sufficient to rely upon in times of pressing need. All of the preceding analysis is according to Rabbi Serayah Deblitzky, may he live long. I then saw a similar approach in the Gesher HaChaim (§3) regarding someone who is ill.

HaTzava KaHalacha takes many elements of the commentators above and applies them to the new situation of our time. If one is confident that one will not make a mistake, and the choice is between *Havineinu* and no prayer at all, one should recite *Havineinu*. HaTzava KaHalacha applies this reasoning to the unique situation facing (Israeli) *poskim* (decisors of Jewish law) today. In the Israeli army, lives are threatened and soliders often must choose between a quick *Havineinu* or no prayer at all, much like the situation in the time of the Mishnah and Gemara.

However, unlike the time of the Mishnah and Gemara, today there is unprecedented familiarity with the text of prayer. Soldiers know the prayer fluently (they study it in grade school or before entering the army), and pray from a prayer book where the entire text is laid out for them, printed together with the inclusions for *Havdalah* and *she'elat geshamim*. This technological innovation creates an even greater reason to be lenient because it effectively eliminates the possibility of mistakes. Technological innovation, *dechak*, and fluency with the prayer come together to create a highly plausible reason to recite *Havineinu*.

We have now explored the discussion of the conflict between the general rules of *Havineinu* and the exception of *dechak*. *Dechak* has been explained as a plausible reason to suspend normative rules of *Havineinu* and has been defined by several examples. In addition, Chayei Adam and HaTzava KaHalacha maintain that all situations of *dechak* warrant recitation of *Havineinu*.

Alternative perspective: reintroducing Rav's version

There is an alternative to *Havineinu* that would provide, in *sha'at ha-dechak*, the opportunity to recite a brief text on the conclusion of Shabbat and festivals and the rainy season. It has been assumed throughout this book that the definition of "condensed version of the *Shemoneh Esreh*" — "*Me'ein Shemoneh Esreh*" — is the *Havineinu* cited by Shmuel (Berachot 29a). However, Rav gave another opinion in the Gemara — a shortened prayer that included a separate abridgement of each blessing within *Shemoneh Esreh*. Rashi interpreted Abaye's curse to be on one who recited Shmuel's version of the abridgment — *Havineinu* — instead of Rav's more complete version. The Gemara's scrutiny of Shmuel's *Havineinu* implies that his version is sufficient, while Rav's, which abridges each of the middle blessings, is obviously preferable.

With this reading, a new alternative arises for prayer at the conclusion of Shabbat and festivals (and during the rainy season) when *Havineinu* should not be said: adding the *Havdalah* prayer (or a request for rain) to Rav's version of an abridgement. Chayei Adam gives the following liturgy text of *Me'ein Shemoneh Esreh* for the conclusion of Shabbat and festivals and the rainy season:

חיי אדם כלל כד הלכות תפלה סעיף לא

יאמר תחלה ג' ראשונות כדרכו ואח"כ במוצ"ש יאמר, אתה חוננתנו למדע
תורתך, ותבדילנו ה' אלהינו בין קודש לחול, בין אור לחשך, בין ישראל
לעמים, בין יום השביעי לששת ימי המעשה, וחננו מאתך כו'. ובחול יאמר
אתה חונן לאדם דעת, חננו מאתך דעה בינה והשכל. ברוך אתה ה' חונן
הדעת. השיבנו אבינו לתורתך, והחזירנו בתשובה שלימה לפניך. ברוך
אתה ה', הרוצה בתשובה. סלח לנו אבינו, כי מוחל וסולח אתה. ברוך
אתה ה', חנון המרבה לסלוח. ראה נא בעניינו וגאלנו מהרה, כי גואל חזק
אתה. בא"י גואל ישראל. רפאנו ה' ונרפא, כי אל מלך רופא נאמן אתה.
בא"י רופא חולי עמו ישראל. ברך עלינו את השנה הזאת, ותן טל ומטר
לברכה על פני האדמה, וברך שנתינו כשנים הטובות. בא"י מברך השנים.
תקע בשופר גדול לחירותנו, וקבצנו יחד מארבע כנפות הארץ. בא"י
מקבץ נדחי עמו ישראל. השיבה שופטינו כבראשונה, ומלוך עלינו אתה
ה' לבדך, וצדקנו במשפט. בא"י מלך אוהב צדקה ומשפט. ולמלשינים אל
תהי תקוה, וכל אויביך מהרה יכרתו, ותכניעם במהרה בימינו. בא"י
שובר אויבים ומכניע זדים. על הצדיקים ועל החסידים ועלינו יהמו
רחמיך, ושים חלקנו עמהם לעולם ולא נבוש, כי בך בטחנו. בא"י משען
ומבטח לצדיקים. ולירושלים עירך ברחמים תשוב, ובנה אותה בקרוב,
וכסא דוד מהרה לתוכה תכין. בא"י בונה ירושלים. את צמח דוד עבדך
מהרה תצמיח, כי לישועתך קוינו כל היום. בא"י מצמיח קרן ישועה. שמע
קולינו וקבל ברחמים וברצון את תפלתנו, כי אל שומע תפלות אתה, בא"י
שומע תפלה. ואח"כ אומר ג' אחרונות ומסיים המברך את עמו ישראל
בשלום. יהיו לרצון כו' עושה שלום כו':

Chayei Adam, Laws of Prayer 24:31

One first says the first three blessings as usual, and then at the
conclusion of Shabbat one says, "You have graciously endowed
us with a knowledge of Your Torah, and have made a
distinction for us, O Lord our God, between sacred and profane,
between light and darkness, between Israel and other nations,
between the seventh day and the six days of work, and
graciously endow us, etc." During the week one says, "You
graciously grant humans knowledge, graciously endow us with
knowledge, wisdom and discernment from You; Blessed are
You, O Lord, gracious giver of knowledge. Return us, our
Father, to Your Torah, and bring us back in complete repentance
before You; Blessed are You, O Lord, who desires repentance.
Forgive us, our Father, for You are one to pardon and forgive;
Blessed are You, O Lord, who is gracious and abundantly
forgives. Look, please, at our affliction, and speedily redeem us,
for you are a mighty redeemer; Blessed are You, O Lord,
redeemer of Israel. Heal us, O Lord, and we shall be healed, for

You are an almighty king and faithful healer; blessed are You, O
Lord, healer of the sick of His people Israel. Bless this year for
us, and send dew and rain as a blessing upon the face of the
earth, and bless our year as the other good years; Blessed are
You, O Lord, who blesses the years. Blow a great shofar to
proclaim our freedom, and gather us together from the four
corners of the earth; Blessed are You, O Lord, who gathers the
dispersed of Your people Israel. Restore our judges as in earlier
times, and reign over us, O Lord, solely, and defend us in
judgment; Blessed are You, O Lord, the king who loves
righteousness and judgment. And for slanderers let there be no
hope, and may all your enemies be speedily cut off, and may
they be brought low speedily in our time; Blessed are You, O
Lord, who destroys the enemies and lowers the wicked. Upon
the righteous and upon the pious and upon us may Your mercy
be aroused, and set our share with them forever, so that we shall
not be put to shame, for we have trusted in You; Blessed are
You, O Lord, the support and haven of the righteous. And to
Jerusalem Your city may You mercifully return, and rebuild it
soon, and speedily prepare the throne of David; Blessed are You,
O Lord, who rebuilds Jerusalem. May You speedily cause the
offshoot of Your servant David to flourish, for we have waited
for Your salvation all the day; Blessed are You, O Lord, who
causes the rays of salvation to flourish. Hear our voices and
mercifully and willingly accept our prayers, for You are a God
who hears prayers; Blessed are You, O Lord, who hears prayers."
Afterward, one says the last there blessings and concludes
with, "Who blesses his nation Israel with peace." "Let [the
words of my mouth] be acceptable, etc." "The One who makes
peace [on high], etc."

Unlike previous authors of halachic codes, Chayei Adam accepts
Rav's condensed prayer as viable and offers this prayer as a
possibility in certain situations. Indeed, it is remarkable that
Chayei Adam raises such a possibility, because although it is
supported by several authorities, the halachic consensus that
developed over numerous centuries seems to have dropped it
from consideration. (In Chapter One, Beit Yosef was cited as
saying "It seems from the Gemara that the halacha is like Shmuel,
as the discussion that follows throughout the chapter speaks of
'Havineinu'; we thus see that this is the way the law is established.
And so have *all* the decisors ruled."[Emphasis added.]) Yet

precisely because he finds that minority stream of interpretation analytically persuasive—or at least sufficiently plausible—Chayei Adam is willing to rely on this version of an abridged *Shemoneh Esreh* in cases of *dechak* when reciting Havineinu is not possible.

Outlines of the various opinions appear in Table 3.9 on page 118.

We have now explored when *Havineinu* may and may not be recited, as set out in traditional sources. With all of our conceptual and practical understanding, we now turn to consider the status of *Havineinu* in our own time.

Table 3.9
Sha'at ha-dechak during the rainy season and at the conclusion of Shabbat and festivals

Options for prayer	Case where it applies	Authority who states this	Comments
Full *Shemoneh Esreh*	When there is only a possibility of outside distractions (*tarud*) Assumes that one will later have the opportunity to complete prayer if stopped in middle	Rabbi Akiva Eiger	This is the case discussed in the Gemara in Berachot 28a.
Havineinu without any insertions	Extreme *dechak* (the time for the prayer is about to end) Only at the conclusion of Shabbat and festivals Choice between *Havineinu* and no prayer at all	Rabbi Akiva Eiger	*Sha'at ha-dechak* equivalent to a *be-de'avad* case and thus has the same rule as one who errs
Rav's version of *Me'ein Shemoneh Esreh* (all middle blessings are condensed)	Extreme *dechak* or ill person Choice between *Havineinu* and no prayer at all	Chayei Adam	Assumes that the Gemara does not reject Rav, but merely accepts the leniency of Shmuel. Against Tur, Rambam and Shulchan Aruch
Mar Zutra's version of *Havineinu* (with special insertions)	If confident that one will not make a mistake Choice between *Havineinu* and no prayer at all	Rabbeinu Manoach Ravad HaTzava KaHalacha	Today we have printed copies of the prayers which contain the added insertions so that familiarity with the additions is assured and safeguard from error is present

Chapter Four
Status of *Havineinu* in modern times

Today, *Havineinu* has fallen into disuse by the general population. There was never any conscious halachic decision to discontinue its use, yet the reality is that *Havineinu* is no longer found in most *siddurim* nor is it well-known by the majority of people who pray. While *Havineinu* was an option for *sha'at ha-dechak*, it has always been preferable to recite the full *Shemoneh Esreh* as instituted by the Sages, and contemporary practice reflects this preference.

The change in practice does not reflect a change in the essential laws of *Havineinu*; rather, it is a difference in application of these laws. For example, one of the goals of *Havineinu* is to ensure proper concentration during prayer. Meiri comments on the importance of this objective:

המאירי בית הבחירה ברכות כח עמוד ב—ל עמוד א
...מוטב שיקצר ויכוין משיאריך ולא יכוין.
Meiri, Beit HaBechirah Commentary to Berachot 28b-30a
...It is better to say less [*Havineinu*] and have *kavvanah* than to say more [the full *Shemoneh Esreh*] and not have *kavvanah*.

While Aruch HaShulchan (Rabbi Yechiel Michel Epstein, 1829-1908) fully agrees with this objective, he questions the ability of *Havineinu* to accomplish its original intent in modern times. He observes a general lack of concentration that is characteristic of all prayer and derives from this that *Havineinu* does not improve concentration levels.

ערוך השולחן אורח חיים סימן קי:ו

אמנם בזמנינו לא שמענו מעולם מי שיתפלל הביננו והטעם פשוט
דבשלמא בימיהם שהיו מכוונים הרבה בתפלה תקנו הביננו לפעמים
כשלא יוכל לכוין אבל האידנא בלא"ה אין אנו מכוונין כל כך כמ"ש כמה
פעמים א"כ למה לנו הביננו.

Aruch HaShulchan, Orach Chaim 110:6
However, in our time, we have never heard of anyone praying *Havineinu*, and the reason is simple: granted in those days, when people were often able to direct their intentions for prayer, [the Sages] instituted *Havineinu* for those times when one was unable to direct one's intentions; but nowadays, we are not so able to direct our intentions for prayer regardless (as I have written numerous times) – if this is the case, what good is *Havineinu*?

Here, Aruch HaShulchan adds an interesting consideration: the ability of the population to have proper intention in prayer. He admits that his contemporaries were unable to maintain sufficient concentration during any prayer. For this reason, *Havineinu* would not improve one's ability to concentrate and is thus rendered useless. Aruch HaShulchan shows that it is possible that a purpose of *Havineinu*—to ensure a level of *kavvanah*—has become unrealizable in modern times.

In addition to *kavvanah*, four other factors have been identified in previous chapters as criteria that might influence one's decision to recite *Havineinu*:

1. Lack of proficiency in prayer.
2. Insufficient knowledge of the laws surrounding *Havineinu*.
3. Presence of danger.
4. Constraints placed on a laborer's time by the employer.

And just as *Havineinu* can no longer be seen as improving one's ability to concentrate on prayer, these factors have become much less significant than in the times of the Mishnah and Gemara.

1. With the advent of widespread availability of the *siddur*, the influence of the first two of these factors have been diminished, if not practically eliminated. Fluency in prayer is virtually irrelevant when the text is readily available and affordable.
2. Most printed *siddurim* have the pertinent laws of prayer printed within, making complete knowledge of the laws of prayer less essential than before. Modern times have also seen an improved schooling system where liturgy and law are better and more widely taught.
3. Routine danger is not a modern reality for the majority of Jews around the world, especially in contemporary America.
4. Work environments on the whole allow for more flexible schedules and are more relaxed than has been the case in the past. Many countries have unions and other methods of protecting workers' rights.

Thus, changes in technology and social circumstances have made it easier, or even more practical, for one to recite the full *Shemoneh Esreh* and have thereby significantly reduced, if not obviated, the need for one to recite *Havineinu*.

While all of the above changes pertain both to the Diaspora and Israel, one important segment of Israeli society does routinely face some of these factors that call for *Havineinu*. The issues of danger and significant constraints on personal time are a living reality for members of the Israeli Army. In a country where the majority of youth are conscripted into the army and where citizens are called to reserve duty, such situations are ever-present. Soldiers are often forced to push prayer aside due to dangerous situations or pressing military needs. Beyond danger, in the army one's time is never one's own and is much more limited even than that of the laborer.

The continuation of the above-cited source addresses this reality in a parenthetical aside:

ערוך השולחן אורח חיים סימן קי:ו
[ומהנכון היה להרגיל לאנשי חיל שנחוצים לעבודתם להתפלל הביננו]:
Aruch HaShulchan, Orach Chaim 110:6
However, it is proper to instruct soldiers who are pressed in
their work to recite *Havineinu.*

Aruch HaShulchan, who in other circumstances does not advocate
reciting *Havineninu* nowadays, notes that soldiers are an exception
to his rule. Today, this practice is common among religious
soldiers in the Israel Defense Forces, and *Havineinu* is included in
most *siddurim* available in Israel, especially those put out by
Religious Zionist presses, such as Koren and Rinat Yisrael.

Unlike Israel, the Diaspora has not significantly encountered
mass army service (at least not since conscription into the Czar's
army), the sole remaining modern impetus for the recitation of
Havineinu.[14] Consequently, one is hard-pressed to find the text of
Havineinu in any contemporary American *siddur* produced for the
Orthodox community. Most notably, *Havineinu* is absent from the
standard-bearing *siddur* of our generation, the ArtScroll Siddur by
Mesorah Publications.

This difference can be readily explained by considering the level
of danger in these respective lands. Danger and pressing need as
constraints on prayer have for all intents and purposes
disappeared in America, but they remain real in contemporary
Israel. While much of this analysis of the reasoning behind this
trend remains speculative, a survey of modern codes of law and
responsa supports the observation that *Havineinu* is falling out of
favor worldwide (save in Israel).

These trends also take time—decades, if not centuries—to
develop. This helps explain why, despite the apparent similarities
of the two societies, most American *siddurim* no longer contain
Havineinu, while many important British *siddurim* still include it.

---

[14] Even during World War II, the last war to see religious Jewish soldiers
serving in large numbers, American soldiers were either in battle and in
great peril (rendering even *Havineinu* unnecessary), or out of theater and in
no danger at all (and required to recite the full *Shemoneh Esreh*); there was
very little middle ground which called for *Havineinu.*

Feelings of security are relative: There has not been a war fought on (densely settled) American soil for nearly two hundred years. But for Britain, memories of the devastation and upheaval during the Blitz are just sixty years old and only now beginning to fade. Thus, in *The Authorised Daily Prayer Book* edited by Dr. Joseph H. Hertz, the late Chief Rabbi of the British Empire, and published right after World War II in 1947, *Havineinu* is printed (page 158) along with the following instructions: "In illness, or when time is lacking, the following shortened form of the *Amidah* may be said." And while newer British *siddurim* still include *Havineinu*, this inclusion likely owes to the continuation of established tradition rather than an appraisal of the need for such a prayer nowadays.[15]

Havineinu becomes an uncommon practice — societal considerations

Within contemporary halachic sources, social reality plays a key role in determining the common practice. As has been described above, with many new factors that obviate the need for *Havineinu* — from better education about laws and prayer to readily available prayer books — *Havineinu* has become nearly ignored in Jewish communities of the West. While these changes do not necessarily eliminate the halachic possibility of reciting *Havineinu*, this abridged prayer offers virtually no advantage to the observant community in latter-day America or Europe. Aside from the reasons mentioned above, modern *poskim* provide several other explanations for why *Havineninu* should or should not be recited.

According to the understanding of Rabbi Akiva's position, *Havineinu* is permitted in situations ranging from an individual with lack of proficiency to *sha'at ha-dechak*. However, Tur only cites a limited set of cases of *sha'at ha-dechak* as reason to recite

---

[15] The latest, fourth edition of *The Authorised Daily Prayer Book of the United Hebrew Congregations of the Commonwealth*, published in 2006 with a new translation and commentary by Chief Rabbi Sir Jonathan Sacks, includes the *Havineinu* prayer on page 96, but with its use circumscribed: "In emergencies and special cases of urgency only, the following shortened form of the *Amidah* may be said (though not when 'Grant dew and rain' is said)."

Havineinu.[16] Aruch HaShulchan notes an important omission, and contends that Tur does not mention situations which have been rendered irrelevant by social and technological change.

ערוך השלחן קי:ג

והטור כתב וה"מ בשעת הדחק כגון שהוא בדרך וכיוצא בו וכשיבא לביתו א"צ לחזור ולתפלל פעם אחרת אבל שלא בשעת הדחק אין לומר אותו עכ"ל ולא הזכיר שקצרה לשונו מלהתפלל אף ע"ג דעיקר פי' המשנה כן הוא נ"ל משום דהאידנא שהנוסחא יש בכל הסידורים לא שייך לומר שקצרה לשונו מהתפלל ורק בזמן הש"ס שהיו מתפללים בע"פ שייך לומר שאין שגורה בפיו ולא בזמה"ז שמתפללים בסידורים.

Aruch HaShulchan 110:3

The Tur wrote, "This applies in a time of pressing circumstances—for instance, when one is traveling and the like—and when one returns home, one need not return and pray another time; but in non-pressing circumstances, one may not say [*Havineinu*]," but he did not mention [the case of] one who has difficulty composing one's prayers (literally, one's tongue is short of prayer), even though this is the main explanation of the Mishnah. It seems to me that [the reason is] because nowadays that the text [of *Shemoneh Esreh*] is found in all prayer books, it is no longer relevant to include one who has difficulty composing one's prayers. Only in Talmudic times, when they prayed by heart, would it be relevant to say that one is not fluent in prayer [lit., prayer does not dwell in one's mouth]—not in our time when we all pray from *siddurim*.

Aruch HaShulchan notes that Tur only mentions traveling as a case of *sha'at ha-dechak*, as opposed to a lack of proficiency in prayer (a factor that is central to Rabbi Akiva's formulation). Tur omits the factor of lack of proficiency in prayer; Aruch HaShulchan explains (somewhat ahistorically) that this concern was eliminated by the advent of printed prayer books. With the widespread use of the *siddur*, the only remaining cause of *sha'at ha-dechak* according to Tur would be travel.

Bi'ur Halacha [Rabbi Israel Meir (HaCohen) Kagan, 1838-1933] recognizes the discrepancy between modern situational realities

---

[16] Tur, Orach Chaim 110[:1].

and the ruling in Shulchan Aruch. Here he resolves the apparent contradiction between performance (i.e., no one reciting *Havineinu* in actuality) and law (i.e., the permissibility of reciting it.)

ביאור הלכה סימן קי

או שלא יוכל וכו' – רצונו לומר מפני רוב טרדותיו או שהוא חולה וכהיום אין נוהגין להתפלל הביננו מחמת הטרדה ונראה לי הטעם לזה דלכאורה קשה על הדין דשולחו ערוך מלעיל סימן ק"א ס"א דאיתא שם דאם אינו יכול לכוין את לבו בכולם יכוין את לבו על כל פנים באבות ומשמע דעל ידי זה ממילא מותר להתפלל כל התפילה כיון שהוא אנוס שאינו יכול לכוין אך דיש לומר דכאן דמיירי דשבעה ברכות יכול לכוין לכך התירו לו להתפלל הביננו ולא יותר כדי שיכלול כל השמונה עשרה בקצרה ובכונה אבל שם מיירי דלא יכול לכוין אפילו אלו הז' ברכות לכך לא התירו לו לקצר על כן ניחא דלא נהגו היום בהביננו שאנו חוששין שאפילו הז' לא יכוין וכענין דכתב הרמ"א שם בס"א בהג"ה...

Bi'ur Halacha, Orach Chaim 110, s.v. *oh*

Or if one is unable, etc. – He [Shulchan Aruch] means to say due to one's excessive encumbrances, or if one is ill. And nowadays our practice is not to say *Havineinu* due to encumbrance. It seems to me that the reason for this comes from the answer to the following question—ostensibly, this law regarding *Havineinu* contradicts the ruling of the Shulchan Aruch above, §101:1, where there it is cited that if one is unable to direct one's heart for all the blessings, one should at least do so for the first blessing. This implies that apparently for this reasoning it is permissible to recite the entire *Shemoneh Esreh* [rather than *Havineinu*], because one is duressed and unable to direct one's attention to prayer. However, one might suggest that here the law is discussing a case where one is able to direct one's attention for the seven blessings; therefore, one is permitted to recite *Havineinu* and not more, so that one may include all of the eighteen blessings concisely but with directed attention. There, though, the law is discussing a case where one is unable to direct one's attention even for the seven blessings [of *Havineinu*]; therefore, one is not permitted to be concise. Consequently, it is now understood that the practice today is not to recite *Havineinu* because we are concerned that one will be unable to direct one's attention even for the seven blessings, similar to what the Rama wrote there in §110:1…

Bi'ur Halacha concludes on two grounds that one should not

recite *Havineinu* nowadays. First, people today are unable to concentrate sufficiently on *Havineinu*. Therefore, one should recite *Shemoneh Esreh*, at the very least concentrating fully on its first blessing – a minimal requirement (see Orach Chaim 101:1). If people are only capable of concentrating on the first blessing, he argues, how could *Havineinu*'s contraction of the middle sections improve concentration?

Bi'ur Halacha offers a second observation:

ביאור הלכה סימן קי ד"ה או שלא (המשך)

...אי נמי מפני שאם באנו לקצר כהיום מחמת טרדה לא נתפלל לעולם
תפילה שלמה מפני רוב הטרדה בעולם הזה:

Bi'ur Halacha, Orach Chaim 110 (continued)
...Or else the reason is because if we would attempt nowadays to recite a concise prayer due to encumbrance, we would never recite a full prayer because of the numerous pressures in this world.

Even though *Havinenu* is the accepted practice in limited circumstances (*sha'at ha-dechak*), due to the "numerous pressures of this world," the applications of this circumstance have grown more prevalent than ever before. Thus, if *Havineinu* were accepted in times of *dechak*, it follows that *Shemoneh Esreh* would fall into disuse.

Kaf HaChaim (Rabbi Yaakov Chaim Sofer, 1870-1939) takes a stricter attitude toward *Havineinu*. In opposition to those whose primary concerns are the social milieu, Kaf HaChaim presents a halachic case for the reason why *Havineinu* has fallen out of use:

כף החיים או"ח קי:ח

וכבר כתבנו לעיל אות ה' דאין נוהגין להתפלל הביננו בזמן הזה ואפילו
בדרך ובשעת הדחק אלא מזרזין עצמן להתפלל בזמנה ובישוב הדעת אם
הם טרודים ואם נאנסי ולא נשאר זמן משלימין בתפילה שאחריה.

Kaf HaChaim, Orach Chaim 110:8
We have already written above (110:5) that the common practice nowadays is no longer to say *Havineinu*, even when traveling and even in a time of pressing need. Rather, people should push themselves to pray at the proper time and with a settled mind

even when encumbered. If circumstances become beyond
people's control and there is no longer time [to pray], they make
up the missed prayer with the following prayer [by performing
tashlumin, a compensatory repetition of *Shemoneh Esreh* during
the next prayer service].

Rather than relying on *Havineinu* in a situation of pressing
circumstances, one should attempt to concentrate on *Shemoneh
Esreh*. If the full *Shemoneh Esreh* is not a viable option at the present
time, it is preferable according to Kaf HaChaim for one to "make
up" the missed prayer by repeating the *Shemoneh Esreh* at the next
prayer service (*tashlumin*), rather than to recite *Havineinu* now. As
the least preferable of several halachic options, *Havineinu* has thus
fallen out of practice entirely.

The authorities above describe why it would be less than ideal to
recite *Havineinu* under so many different conditions, or even why
one should not recite it at all. Accordingly, these positions result
in infrequent recitation of this prayer (if ever). Ironically, then,
even if one were to find oneself in a sitation that these
commentators would sanction reciting *Havineinu*, one would
likely be so unfamiliar with this prayer that its time-saving
advantage over *Shemoneh Esreh* would be lost. Rabbi Moshe
Feinstein (Iggrot Moshe, 1895-1986) notes this explicitly:

שו"ת אגרות משה חלק או"ח ד סימן צא (ב)

אם רשאין לדלג פסוקי דזמרה כשיתאחר בשביל זה המלמד להתחיל
ללמד עם התלמידים ופועל השכור למלאכתו ולמלאכת עצמו ולדלג
פסד"ז כפי שאיתא (שו"ע או"ח) בסימן נ"ב לא בשביל תפלה בצבור,
אלא שהוא מלמד ואיחר מלקום כשיתפלל בלא דלוג לא יוכל לבא לתחלת
הזמן שצריך להתחיל ללמד עם התלמידים, ולפעמים כדי שיספיק לאכול
איזה דבר שלא יהיה רעב בשעת למודו עם התלמידים שלא ילמוד עמהם
כראוי, פשוט וברור שצריך לדלג, שהרי בזה איכא תרתי בטול תורה
דהתינוקות וחיוב הפעולה שהוא ענין גזל. ואף כשהוא שכיר לאחרים
לעניני הרשות נמי מחוייב לדלג אם איחר שלא יוכל לבא בזמן התחלת
המלאכה, דהוא ענין גזל מלאכתו דבעה"ב, והא הקלו לפועלים אף לר"ג
שיתפללו רק מעין י"ח דהוא הבינונו ושיברכו רק שתים בברכת המזון
לאחריה ומסתמא שלא היו אומרין כלל פסד"ז, ולכן אף שהאידנא
מתפללין י"ח ומברכין בהמ"ז כתקונה מחמת שאין דרך להקפיד בכך
ואדעתא דהכי משכירין אותן כדאיתא בסימן ק"י סעי' ב' ובסימן קצ"א

סעי' ב', לא שייך זה בצריך לבא למלאכתו בשעה מיוחדת כפועלים
בזמננו ואירע שנתאחר, ודאי אין רשאי על זמן בעה"ב להאריך בתפלתו
והיה לו להתפלל בעצם הביננו כמו שהוא בדרך וכן לברך רק שתי ברכות
בבהמ"ז כשיהיה הפסד לבעה"ב אף כשינכה לו שכרו, אך למעשה
מסתבר שאין לעשות כן, לא מבעיא לחסר ברכה בבהמ"ז דבשביל מקרה
כזה אין לשנות, אלא אף בתפלת הביננו שבדרך רשאי גם בזמננו, אבל
כיון שלא רגיל בהביננו ואינו בקי בה לא ירויח אלא משהו ואולי לא
ירויח כלל...

Iggrot Moshe, Orach Chaim 4:91(2)

[Rabbi Feinstein discusses different alternatives for a
schoolteacher or employee to shorten his prayer—such as
skipping *Pesukei DeZimrah* (Verses of Praise). One must decrease
the time it takes them to pray in certain circumstances, he says,]
because this (i.e., taking too much time away from work) is a
matter of theft of labor belonging to the employer. And [in the
Talmud (Berachot 16a)] we find lenient rulings for laborers: even
according to Rabban Gamliel they should recite only a
condensed version of *Shemoneh Esreh*, which is *Havineinu*, and
should say only two blessings of the Grace after Meals, and
presumably they did not say *Pesukei DeZimrah* at all. Therefore,
even though nowadays laborers say the full *Shemoneh Esreh* and
say the Grace after Meals as it was established, because the
practice is not to be particular about these matters and
employers hire with this in mind, as cited in §110:2 and §191:2,
this has no bearing on the need to arrive at work at a specific
time—like employees in our times—and if it turns out that one is
late, certainly one is not permitted to pray extensively on the
employer's time. In such a case, one should really have said
Havineinu, just as one does when traveling, and also to have said
only two blessings of the Grace after Meals, when a loss to the
employer is involved, even when one's pay is reduced
accordingly; however, in practice, one might persuasively argue
not to do this—not only regarding skipping blessings from Grace
after Meals, for in a case like this one should not deviate from
the accepted practice—but even with regard to *Havineinu*, which
is still permitted to travelers nowadays, but since one is not used
to saying *Havineinu* and not expert in it, one gains very little by
saying it, perhaps nothing at all!....[17]

---

[17] Rabbi Feinstein concludes:

שו"ת אגרות משה חלק חו"ח ד סימן צא (המשך)
וא"כ לדלג פסד"ז ודאי לא מיבעיא שרשאי אלא שמחוייב מצד גזל מלאכתו של בעה"ב. אך

Rabbi Feinstein considers many of the issues previously discussed in this book, such as theft from the employer and *sha'at ha-dechak*. While acknowledging that there is an obligation of an employee to an employer ("certainly one is not permitted to pray extensively on the employer's time") and the legitimacy of reciting an abridged prayer in such a circumstance ("in such a case one should really have said *Havineinu*, just as one does when traveling"), he concludes that because *Havineinu* is no longer recited generally, one need not recite it in this case either. Rabbi Feinstein makes his ruling based on the assumption that people are more adept with *Shemoneh Esreh* than with the unfamiliar *Havineinu*. This assumption is the exact opposite of the Gemara's original supposition, that the concise prayer will save time. No longer a useful, time-saving abridgement, *Havineinu* actually consumes more time and is a greater burden than the longer, more familiar *Shemoneh Esreh*. Even though practice is now different than the times of the Gemara, the halacha itself never changed. Rabbi Feinstein still permits use of *Havineinu* in certain situations, namely by travelers. Of course, as Rabbi Feinstein implies, were people to become more familiar with the text of *Havineinu*, it would revert to being a viable option.

The reasons given for not reciting *Havineinu* are numerous, and they take into account factors such as technology, social practice, and the consequences of always reciting it. Aruch HaShulchan argues that because of the prayer book, there is no need for *Havineinu*, as everyone is proficient in *Shemoneh Esreh*. He also observes the social climate—the general ability to concentrate has declined—and notes that, accordingly, there is no reason to recite *Havineinu* because its objective would still not be met. Bi'ur

---

בשביל מלאכת עצמו מסתבר שלא ידלג אלא כשאיכא חשש גדול שאפשר יהיה הפסד
כשיאחר זמן הקצר דאמירת כל פסד"ז דבמקום הפסד ודאי רשאי אף למלאכת עצמו.

Iggrot Moshe, Orach Chaim 4:91(2) (continued)

Therefore, certainly there is no question that one is *permitted* to skip *Pesukei DeZimrah*; rather, one *must* do so to avoid theft of labor belonging to the employer. However, for the loss of one's own labor, it would seem that one may not skip [*Pesukei DeZimrah*] unless there is a great concern that a loss will result from being late the short time it takes to say all of *Pesukei DeZimrah*, for in a case of loss one is certainly permitted [to skip], even for one's own labor.

Halacha continues this line of thought, arguing that if we are unable to concentrate on one blessing (which is minimally required), how could we be capable of concentrating on seven? He also notes that the nature of pressing situations has changed over time: rather than the *dechak* of perilous situations such as travel, religious Jews in the modern era face the more mundane increased pressures of everyday life. And since ordinary life is so hectic, were we to rule that we should recite *Havineinu* in every case of *sha'at ha-dechak* nowadays, we would simply recite *Havineinu* all the time. Such a ruling could well generate the absurd situation in which the full *Shemoneh Esreh* would never be recited at all! Finally, Iggrot Moshe observes that though *Havineinu* was intended to be a less cumbersome prayer, nowadays it has become more of a burden because it has fallen into disuse.

Havineinu as common practice: the situation of Israeli soldiers

Two reasons for the contemporary practice not to recite *Havineinu*—unfamiliarity with the prayer such that it loses its comparative time advantage over *Shemoneh Esreh*, and the change in the nature of the pressures that people face from true peril to the more mundane stresses of everyday life—are not in fact universal. The dangers faced today in Israel, particularly by members of the Israel Defense Forces, are grave and real. The conditions of peril and hazard that gave rise to the need for the *Havineinu* prayer centuries ago, and which gradually receded, have returned. Religious soldiers not only need to recite *Havineinu*, but they are trained to do so, such that they have revived its advantage over the full *Shemoneh Esreh*. They also recite (or practice) *Havineinu* enough not to have any misconceptions about the prayer. Even the Aruch HaShulchan's point about technology has come full circle—the widespread availability of printed copies of *Havineinu* in *siddurim* and handbooks for Israeli soldiers has made Havineinu a more viable option.

הצבא כהלכה: הלכות מלחמה וצבא פרק מ"ג

בשעת דחק גדולה, אפשר להתפלל "שמונה עשרה" בנוסח "ברכת הבינינו" (כגון שהוא בדרך, או שהיה עומד במקום שהוא טרוד וירא שיפסיקוהו, או שלא יוכל להתפלל בכוונה תפילה ארוכה), גם בימות

הגשמים ומוצאי שבת.
HaTzava KaHalacha: Hilchot Milchamah veTzava (R. Yitzchak Kofman, 1992) Ch. 43
In cases of great pressing need, one may recite *Shemoneh Esreh* with the text of *Havineinu* (for example, if one is traveling, or one is standing in a place where one is encumbered and afraid of being interrupted, or one is unable to direct one's intention for a full-length prayer), even during the rainy season or at the conclusion of Shabbat.

Other halachic guides for soldiers also rule that *Havineinu* can be an alternative for *Shemoneh Esreh*, though with further limitations:

דיני צבא ומלחמה, הל' תפילה: תפילה בשעת הדחק

תפילת "הביננו" נאמרת במקום שמונה עשרה, בעמידה, ורק בקיץ, כי אין בה שאלת טל ומטר. (ק"י,א). נוסח הביננו הוא זה: הביננו ה' אלהינו לדעת דרכיך...

אין אומרים "הביננו" במוצאי שבתות וימים טובים, כי אי אפשר להוסיף בהם "אתה חוננתנו" (ק"י,א).

Dinei Tzava u-Milchamah (Rabbi Shlomo Min HaHar, Yissachar Golman and Yehuda Eisenberg, 2001, Rev. ed.), Laws of Prayer
The *Havineinu* prayer is said while standing in place of *Shemoneh Esreh*. It is said only in the summertime, when there is no request for dew and rain (Orach Chaim 110:1). [Quotes the text of *Havineinu*.]
One may not say *Havineinu* at the conclusion of Shabbat and festivals, for at those times it is not possible to add the text of *Havdalah* (Orach Chaim 110:1).

In the Israeli army, soldiers are familiar with the prayer and have ready access to *siddurim* which lay out the full text of *Havineinu*, including the blessings before and after. Indeed, as part of their preparation before entering the army, religious students are taught a mnemonic tune for *Havineinu*, a conscious effort to make it more familiar to them when needed. In such a case, where the prayer is familiar and texts are available, *Havineinu* becomes a much more viable option.

Summary of contemporary practice: two distinct situations

Havineinu has always been regarded as a leniency, one which—as many decisors remind us—we should be careful not to abuse. Although created in order to help one concentrate on prayer within trying circumstances, the use of this prayer can potentially be abused. As stated above, Bi'ur Halacha fears that people might come to rely solely on *Havineinu*, to the exclusion of the *Shemoneh Esreh*.

Despite these hesitancies, there is now a situation that calls for the revival of *Havineinu*—namely, service in the Israeli Army. Permitting the recitation of *Havineinu* in this situation does not constitute a violation of or change in halacha. Rather, the needs of the situation called for revisiting the corpus of Jewish law texts, honestly analyzing and interpreting the sources, and reviving a possibly dormant line of thinking within the tradition—that is, reconsidering an opinion or opinions that may once again prove relevant. This process is the essence of innovation in Jewish law.

Chapter Five
Conclusion

Though Torah is God-given, halacha is neither static nor stagnant; rather, it demands human involvement. Active study and participation in deriving the halacha from the Rabbinic sources are fundamental components of the halachic process. These endeavors often produce unexpected conclusions—this is the essence of *chiddush*. As we have seen throughout this book, halacha largely changes through *chiddush*—the innovative interpretation of sources.

A variety of factors, both internal and external to halachic texts, drive intellectual innovation. Every legal system inherently requires study and interpretation, which lead to incremental changes within the law. As more study occurs, further understandings of and approaches to the law are developed, and ultimately, the law undergoes more change. Partly as a result of the religious responsibility to study and understand Jewish law that is embraced by its adherents, Jewish law has undergone an intensely deep and broad investigation and exploration. Jewish law contains a large corpus of complex laws, including ambiguous and inconclusive primary texts, and a multiplicity of approaches to understanding its concepts. Against the backdrop of these and many other factors, the *posek* (decisor) seeks to understand and apply the law. New ideas often result in modification—by way of expansion or limitation—of a concept. External factors that drive *chiddush* include changes in society, technology, and economic conditions. As reality changes, the principles of a particular halacha must be analyzed again and appropriately applied to the new situation.

The religious need to study and understand the primary texts of Jewish law is self-evident, and this intrinsic need drives change. While *poskim* (decisors) universally aim to explore the concepts behind rules, their approaches differ. For example, when faced with a contradiction—between two sources, among several commentaries, or between practice and law—*poskim* exhibit two primary approaches: "harmonization," where a *posek* rereads the text(s) to minimize and resolve contradictions, and "ruling," where a *posek* simply accepts one opinion over another. Of course, some *poskim* stake out a middle ground, at times using each of these two methods, leading to a more complex understanding of the law.

The **initial section** of this chapter will explain why change is inherent in all law systems, and then reintroduce the arguments and conceptual developments within the discussion of *Havineinu* that exemplify this reality. Throughout this presentation, the elements of *chiddush* will be highlighted, and contradictions will be discussed as impetuses for *chiddush*. **Section two** will explore the two broad categories of approaches to contradictions and show that any effort to confront contradictions results in a degree of change. **Section three** shifts focus from *chiddushim* generated in the study hall as a result of conceptual analysis to those that develop as a result of a changing reality filled with technological advances and sociological shifts. It addresses the question, "What happens when the circumstances that a halacha originally addressed are no longer prevalent?" The **fourth section** takes a step back and looks at the broader changes that exist in the practiced halacha to answer the question, "What has changed in the ruling about *Havineinu* over time, and what is the range of rulings between authorities?" The **fifth and final section** of this chapter will ask and answer the question, "So what, in the end, changes with *chiddush*?" Here, it will be shown that *chiddush* is not a radical, conscious change of the law. Rather, it is the subtle adjustment of understanding behind the law. While the technical reasoning employed in interpreting a source may be novel and the ramifications may affect practice, fundamentally, the halacha itself has not changed.

5.1 Inherent change

It is a long recognized truth that law texts, by their very nature, require study and continual interpretation. The necessity of these actions stems from the internal ambiguities and at times opaque nature of rulings that are inherent to complex legal documents. Inevitably, incremental changes result from these interpretations. Living law codes have additional impetuses for interpretation, including attempts to apply the law to specific cases or to incorporate previously unaccounted for situations and circumstances into the law code.

To a greater extent than most law codes, basic Jewish law sources—among them the Mishnah and Gemara—present interpreters with further difficulties, rendering innovative interpretation absolutely essential. Although they form the foundation of halacha, these basic texts are not structured as, or intended to be, a legal code in the traditional sense. Rather, rulings are established based on case law, in which laws are presented not as hard and defined rules, but through the context of specific cases. This type of presentation will often result in general statements based on specific cases without caveats stipulated for the numerous exceptions that remain unaccounted for. Often, even when it appears that all cases are covered by a law, new situations develop, leaving the law as written unequipped to account for them. It is, therefore, the responsibility of the legal commentators and decisors to abstract the cases in the Gemara in order to create universal rules and laws. Because the underlying concepts and principles must be separated from the details of each specific case, this process requires a great amount of precision and care. This form of interpretation is crucial in extending the application of the law to new cases. Another impetus for interpretation is the frequent lack of conclusive rulings. A third driving force behind *chiddush* is the sheer size of the corpus of Jewish texts. Often, secondary texts—because of their supplementary or contradictory material—compel a new reading of a main text. Decisors must also deal with the various interpretations of halachic commentators when their opinions seem contradictory. Clearly, interpretation is inherent within halacha; it is a necessary and natural process, not a conscious, unbounded act of modification.

Internal ambiguity and inconclusive rulings

While Mishnaic discussions and Talmudic passages sometimes conclude with explicit rulings or rejections of opinions, most often they do not. Frequently, these texts contain a multiplicity of conflicting tannaitic and amoraitic viewpoints with no apparent resolution. The Mishnah that forms the foundation of the discussion of *Havineinu* is one such example. Here, three distinct positions are presented—and yet, in one form or another, later commentators find ways to attribute each with the final ruling of *Havineinu*. Some positions—including Bach—rule in accordance with Rabban Gamliel's statement that "every day a person recites eighteen blessings (*Shemoneh Esreh*);" Eshkol rules like Rabbi Yehoshua—"a condensed version of the eighteen blessings (*Me'ein Shemoneh Esreh*);" and Meiri attributes the law of *Havineinu* to Rabbi Akiva—"if prayer is very familiar to him (literally, dwells upon his lips), he should recite eighteen blessings; if not, [he should recite] a condensed version of the eighteen (*Me'ein Shemoneh Esreh*)." Additionally, some commentators express the final halacha as a combination of Rabban Gamliel's and Rabbi Yehoshua's positions.

Inconclusive rulings are only one of the difficulties that *poskim* confront in Jewish legal writings. Often, a Talmudic text will contain ambiguous phrases or passages. What is the text of *Me'ein Shemoneh Esreh* supported by Rabbi Yehoshua in the Mishnah? Two possibilities are offered in the Gemara: Rav or Shmuel's versions. The only indication of a ruling is Abaye's curse. The meaning of the statement "Abaye curses one who recites *Havineinu*" is unclear, and it is therefore subject to debate among halachic commentaries. The lack of clear evidence in a case leaves a rabbinic commentator to infer the original intent of a ruling, but without an explicit text for support. Rashi bases his interpretation of Abaye's curse on the phrase's context, while Tosafot's explanation is influenced by a consideration of outside sources. Rashi considers this curse to be a reflection of Abaye's preference for Rav's longer abridgment over Shmuel's more condensed version. Tosafot, on the other hand, consider Abaye's curse to refer only to a particular situation—in the city, rather than in the field. It is the ambiguity of the Gemara's statement that allowed for such a wide range of interpretation.

In the Gemara in Berachot 16a, three Baraitot are presented—one instructs laborers to recite a full *Shemoneh Esreh*, a second calls for laborers to recite an abridged version of *Shemoneh Esreh*, and a third draws a distinction between different types of laborers for Grace after Meals. Although the Gemara itself discusses and proposes a resolution to the contradiction between the first two Baraitot, it does not discuss the function of the third Baraita. Rosh and Rif, in their halachic restatements of the Talmud, consider the third Baraita's role as detracting from, rather than supporting, the Gemara's earlier conclusion. Rashi, among others, considers the third Baraita a clear support and precedent for the Gemara's earlier conclusion. Thus, the ambiguity of the purpose of this Baraita leads to diverse readings of this Gemara. Ultimately, these readings lead to differences in ruling. Many following the line of thought put forth by Rif and Rosh and consider *sha'at ha-dechak*, a principal established within a different context, as the sole category of situations that allow one to recite *Havineinu*. Others, following Rashi's approach, codify the case of the laborers as a separate and valid example of a situation necessitating the use of *Havineinu*.

Sometimes commentators make vague or unclear statements, which are, in turn, variously interpreted by later authorities. An example is the explanation given by Talmid Rabbeinu Yonah on Berachot 29a (19b in Rif pagination):

תלמיד ר' יונה ברכות כט עמוד א (יט עמוד ב בדפי הרי"ף)

... ואפשר לומר טעם בדבר דמשום הכי לא תקינו מעין הבדלה מפני
שההבדלה אינה ברכה בפני עצמה אלא שאנו כוללים אותה בברכת אתה
חונן ואם היו אומרים מעין הבדלה היה נראה שההבדלה היא ברכה בפני
עצמה כיון שהתקינו מעין הבדלה כמו שתקנו מעין שאר ברכות.

Talmid Rabbeinu Yonah, Berachot 29a (19b in Rif pagination)

...Perhaps one could offer a reason...[the Sages] did not institute
an abstraction of *Havdalah* because the *Havdalah* is not an
independent blessing; rather, it is included in the blessing of
Atah Chonein (Who grants wisdom)—and if we were to allow an
abstraction of *Havdalah*, it would appear as if *Havdalah* were an
independent blessing, since [the sages] instituted an abstraction
of *Havdalah* just as they instituted an abstraction of the other
blessings.

Although he explicitly rules that *Havdalah* cannot be added into
Havineinu because it would appear as a separate blessing,
Rabbeinu Yonah does not specify what case this concern affects.
Bach and Perishah remain free to interpret the original intent.
They each take a slightly different approach in understanding
Rabbeinu Yonah—Bach focuses on the laws of *Havineinu*, and
Perishah focuses on the thematic content.

In his attempt to understand the text, each commentator shapes
the understanding of the underlying concepts and alters the
potential perspectives toward the issues. When Tosafot read
Abaye's curse as applying to situations in the city, they allow
other commentators to expand this definition to include elements
of confusion, concentration and time into their formulations.
Ambiguous phrases and passages, as well as inconclusive rulings,
require explanation and interpretation. The solutions to the
problems that these types of ambiguous content raise are neither
simple nor straightforward. Texts of this type by their very nature
allow for a range of approaches and a variety of understandings.
Thus, while commentaries "do change" a concept from a previous
understanding, these commentaries actually provide a necessary,
though innovative, form of clarification.

Case law, rules, and rationale

Internal ambiguities and inconclusive rulings are a direct result of the unique presentation of Jewish law. Mishnah, Baraita, Tosefta, and Gemara are not intended as final legal codes that offer decisive rulings for all cases. Rather, much of their content is dedicated to a presentation of multiple opinions on a given subject or a multiplicity of cases exemplifying the application of the law. Other sections in these works, primarily the Gemara, are intended to investigate the underpinnings of laws—and they do so through a series of logical arguments, with a stream of back-and-forth discourse, and by incorporating other sources. As these elements often make the texts less clear and provide a mass of information to take into account, they do not make the texts amenable to straightforward rulings. Among the ramifications of the Gemara's style are cases of contradictory material, a frequent lack of conclusive rulings, and instances of incomprehensive rulings. Despite all the difficulties encountered in studying these texts, these sources should not, and must not, be viewed as impenetrable or incomprehensible. Their content, while often enigmatic, must ultimately be translated into legal praxis.

The Aggadah about Rabbi Yose's experience with praying in an abandoned synagogue provides a prime example of how laws can be extrapolated from a story. Here, the Gemara itself identifies the laws that can be learned from Rabbi Yose having been chastised by Elijah for stopping his journey to pray in synagogue ruins. "I learned [from my experience] that one does not enter ruins, and that one prays on the road, and that one who prays on the road recites a shortened prayer." Tosafot then take these laws and apply them to the understanding of Abaye's curse.

Often, the nature of case law is such that while the law on a particular situation is given, no rationale behind this ruling is provided. Rather, the underlying elements of a case or list of cases must be abstracted to a general ruling. Rif's commentary, that *Havineinu* may be recited when "one [is] traveling through a wilderness, and similar situations," exemplifies this aspect. Though Rif provides a list of examples, he still leaves the reader free to extrapolate from these cases a general conception of what constitutes "similar situations."

In trying to discern the nature of *Havineinu*, commentators look toward the list of rules for comparing *Havineinu* and *tefillah ketzarah* and try to derive general constructs. The Gemara states that if one recites *Havineinu*, there is no obligation to pray again when reaching one's destination, whereas if one recited *tefillah ketzarah*, one is required to pray again. Rabbeinu Yonah looks at this case and, in particular, at the wording 'arriving at one's destination,' and he concludes that the laws being discussed here apply to a traveler. Going beyond this analysis, Rabbeinu Yonah forms a more general ruling based on this case: *Havineinu* is recited while traveling. Rabbeinu Yonah's explanation expands the utility of the *Havineinu* prayer, and sheds light on its purpose.

Often, case law makes broad, general claims, without detailing the exceptions to its rules. When the Gemara outlines the situations where recitation of *Havineinu* is proscribed, no caveats permit its recitation by ill individuals or by people pressured due to time constrains. Yet Chayei Adam and Magen Avraham clearly distinguish these exceptions to the rule. As Chayei Adam rules, "In a time of pressing need—e.g., ... one is ill—one recites the first three blessings and then says an abstraction of *Shemoneh Esreh*."

Ultimately, the difficulties within the text—including ambiguous phrases, inconclusive rulings, and the need to extrapolate a rationale behind rulings—lead to interpretation and adaptation within Jewish law. Like these types of texts, contradictory sources—or sources which are related thematically but do not directly discuss the same issues—require interpretation.

5.2 Two approaches to contradictions: harmonizing versus ruling

Chiddush is limited by fidelity to the tradition and the classical texts of Jewish law—Talmud, commentaries, treatises, *responsa*, and codes. The continual responsibility of commentators and halachic authorities is to study, infer, and apply the law. When approaching these texts, they strive to maintain the texts' original intent. Simultaneously, *poskim* work toward a continual development and refinement of their understanding of the concepts presented within the works of their predecessors. This involves reading, interpreting, and weighing the texts as part of the faithful search for the truth. Essentially, there are two prevalent approaches to contradictions: one, aiming to eliminate any contradictions between texts and opinions by harmonizing the sources, and two, logically building an argument for one text and downplaying, or possibly rejecting, the others. The first method of approaching the contradictions—harmonization—either minimizes the conflict among sources by drawing key distinctions about the topics or situations addressed in each or, alternatively, by arguing that all sources fit into a single overarching analytic framework. The second method—ruling—resolves contradictions by accepting the validity of certain arguments or sources over others based on appeal to reason.

While these methods display a fundamental commitment to the sources' original intent, they also allow for the continued development of ideas within halacha. Attempting to harmonize multiple sources produces a more unified interpretation of the law, which also results in a new understanding and explanation of the ideas. A similar type of change occurs as well when a *posek* issues a ruling: the process of rationally approaching a text and accepting only one opinion as correct causes a significant change from the previous interpretation.

When addressing the Gemara in Berachot 16a, which deals with the laborer's obligation to recite *Havineinu*, commentators are faced with the question of how to combine this source with the Gemara in Berachot 29a, which establishes the concept of *sha'at ha-dechak*. A simple reading suggests that Rambam chooses to avoid this difficulty; he simply rules in accordance with the distinction between laborers suggested in the Gemara (this places Rambam's codification in direct conflict with the opinion of Rif and Rosh). Yet Tur explains Rambam's view with the principal of *sha'at ha-dechak*. Bach seeks to harmonize Rambam, Tur, Rif, and Rosh, with one unified approach to the concept. While Bach views all sources as equally important, Taz resolves the conflict of

Havineinu by choosing one text over the other. Taz does not ignore a text, nor does he attempt to incorporate all the sources. Instead, he resolves any possible contradiction by explaining why there is none. Taz thinks it obvious that "accept[ing] the 'distinction of pressing circumstances'," a concept not even mentioned in the Gemara in connection to *Havineinu*, "to the exclusion of all others" is "the Gemara's ultimate conclusion" and that "this is the way the halacha is established." Based on what he considers to be the subject of each Talmudic passage, he weighs the texts' importance, and simply considers one to be more important to the discussion of *Havineinu* than the other.

The significance of Bach's commentary is not only that he has explained two, seemingly incongruous, approaches to the Gemara Berachot 16a within the same framework of interpretation. Although in his commentary on *Havineinu* Bach seems to be coming closer to a unified reading, there are many changes that his commentary introduces. The first resolution ascribes one Baraita to Rabban Gamliel and the other to Rabbi Yehoshua. The Gemara itself asks on this "If so, according to Rabbi Yehoshua, why does the Baraita restrict the recitation of a condensed eighteen blessings to laborers? It should be the case for all people!" Whereas on an initial reading it would seem that the Gemara rules against the second interpretation of the Baraitot, Bach's ultimate conclusion is otherwise. Bach argues that the second resolution (i.e., both Baraitot are in accordance with Rabban Gamliel) is weak (because this answer is contradicted by the third Baraita). Going against the apparent flow of the Gemara's argument, Bach seeks to revive the first, and seemingly rejected, resolution. In doing so, he uses a suggestion made and rejected by Tosafot:

תוספות מסכת ברכות דף טז עמוד א ד"ה אפילו כל אדם נמי

...אין זה שום חדוש אם הפועלים אומרים אפילו לכתחלה.

Tosafot, Berachot 16a, s.v. afilu
...there is no novelty in positing that laborers [in addition to everyone else] recite such a version [because this fact is already obvious], even *ab initio (lechatchilah)*.

Although Tosafot clearly state "there is no novelty" in attributing

the second Baraita in Berachot 16a to Rabbi Yehoshua, Bach uses
their commentary as a support for just such a suggestion:

ב"ח אורח חיים קי:ד (המשך)

...לאו קושיא היא כלל דכל אדם ודאי רשות הוא להתפלל מעין י"ח לר'
יהושע אבל פועלים חובה הוא עליהן להתפלל מעין י"ח שלא לבטל
ממלאכת בעל הבית כמו שהקשו התוספות...

Bach, Orach Chaim 110:4 (continued)
[There] is no question at all: for all people, it is clearly optional
to recite a condensed version of the *Shemoneh Esreh* according to
Rabbi Yehoshua, but for laborers it is incumbent upon them to
recite the condensed version in order that they not be
[exceedingly] idle from the landlord's work—as Tosafot posited
in their question...

While Tosafot state that there is no novelty in ascribing the
second Baraita to Rabbi Yehoshua, Bach suggests one based on
the obligation to recite *Shemoneh Esreh*. Thus, even though Bach
takes the harmonizing approach in trying to eliminate any
contradictions between commentaries, he does produce a shift in
the understanding of the Gemara.

Bach's method of harmonization is to apply one line of reasoning
to many sources and to assume that they all work with the same
assumptions and view of the Gemara. In confronting
contradictory sources, a second method of harmonization exists—
minimizing the area of contradiction. Instead of understanding
the two sources as addressing the same situation, a subtle
distinction can be drawn between them. When discussing the
Gemara in Berachot 29a, wherein Mar Zutra proposes
incorporating *Havdalah* and *she'elat geshamim* into *Havineinu*,
Tosafot bring in another Gemara. Although this Gemara in
Niddah 8b does not contradict the source in Berachot outright,
Tosafot are troubled by the following difficulty. The situation of a
congregation on the conclusion of Shabbat or festivals and that of
a congregation at the conclusion of Yom Kippur are similar—they
may be impelled to recite *Havineinu*, but this prayer does not
include the necessary *Havdalah* insertions. Yet, Tosafot note, in
only one of these contexts is Mar Zutra's suggested inclusion
mentioned. In order to account for this inconsistency, Tosafot

marginalize the area of contradiction by attributing each Gemara to a separate situation—the congregation discussed in Berachot is familiar with *Havineinu*, while the congregation in Niddah is not. And, in order to preserve daily practice, namely the regular recitation of *Havineinu*, Mar Zutra's proposal is brought up in the appropriate context. Thus, even though the Gemara does not mention community practice when discussing the appropriateness of *Havineinu* in different contexts, Tosafot propose this resolution. Their reading indeed has practical ramifications: in contemporary times, when virtually no community recites *Havineinu*, many *poskim*, including Iggrot Moshe, discourage its recitation.

5.3 Changes in reality

The development from cases and lists to regulations and laws requires an understanding of what the cases and lists exemplify. Because these rules have at their foundation a rationale, even once a firm rule is established, when a specific rationale no longer applies in a particular circumstance, the ruling is overturned in that specific case. But when the rationale applies once again, the practice will become revived. What causes a specific rationale to no longer apply is not changes in logical understanding, or even an individual's approach to the text. Rather, a change in reality alters the relevance and applicability of a certain law.

Even in the case of prayer, an area of halacha that is less susceptible than most to change and the influence of technology, a change in practice has occurred over time and between different communities. This change did not occur arbitrarily, but rather had its basis in an understanding of the law.

From the technical distinction drawn between *Havineinu* and *tefillah ketzarah* about sitting or standing during prayer, Rosh derives that *Havineinu* is suited for a situation where maintaining *kavvanah* is difficult. By abstracting a specific rule—one must pray while reciting *Havineinu*—to a general rationale behind the rule—that *Havineinu* is meant for circumstances where one's ability to concentrate is otherwise limited—Rosh creates the intellectual basis for the law's future transformation. When the underlying goal of the law—to preserve concentration—is no longer accomplished by this law, such as when concentration is enhanced by other means such as the *siddur*, or when *Havineinu* is so unfamiliar to the population that it is no longer helpful, the law will fall into disuse. Aruch HaShulchan follows this logic in his ruling. Starting with Rambam's restatement of Rabbi Akiva's formulation—that *Havineinu* is recited when one has difficulty composing his prayers (literally, one's tongue is short of prayer)—he concludes:

ערוך השולחן אורח חיים סימן קי סעיף ג

...נ"ל משום דהאידנא שהנוסחא יש בכל הסידורים לא שייך לומר שקצרה לשונו מהתפלל ורק בזמן הש"ס שהיו מתפללים בעל פה שייך לומר שאין שגורה בפיו ולא בזמה"ז שמתפללין בסידורים.

Aruch HaShulchan, Orach Chaim 110:3

...It seems to me that [the reason *Havineinu* is not recited in situations where there is a lack of familiarity with prayer is] because nowadays the text [of *Shemoneh Esreh*] is found in all prayer books, [and] it is no longer relevant to include one who has difficulty composing one's prayers [among the factors that allows one to recite *Havineinu*]. Only in Talmudic times, when they prayed by heart, is it relevant to say that the prayer does not dwell in one's mouth—not in our time when we all pray from *siddurim*.

This conceptual idea that *siddurim* reduce confusion is found elsewhere as well. In Magen Avraham's commentary on Kohanim offering both the Priestly Blessing and leading the congregation, he writes:

מגן אברהם סימן קכח ס"ק לא

מובטח שיחזור - ולדידן שמתפללין מתוך הסידור מובטח שיחזור לתפלתו ומ"מ כשיש כהנים אחרים לא יעקור רגליו [ל"ח]... ובנ"ץ כתוב שסומכין על שמתפללין מתוך הסידור... לכן נ"ל דבמקום שאין מנהג לא ישא כפיו אם יש כהנים אחרים וכדעת כל הגאונים.

Magen Avraham, Orach Chaim 128:31

Certain that he will be able to return – and for us, who pray from a printed text, we are always certain that the leader will be able to return to his prayers [without becoming confused]. Nevertheless, when there are other Kohanim present [i.e., another viable option besides relying on the printed text] one should not move one's feet [to prepare to offer the Blessing] (source: Lechem Chamudot). [Magen Avraham continues to discuss other approaches to this issue.] Nachalat Tzvi wrote that [the current practice] relies on the fact that we now pray from printed texts. [Magen Avraham continues by disputing the legitimacy of this claim on various grounds, but he concludes that] it appears to me that wherever there is no set custom, the leader should not offer the Priestly Blessing if other Kohanim are present, in accordance with all the great decisors.

Without an understanding of the underpinnings of a law, the proper application of that law cannot take place. Thus, because *poskim* have a firm grasp on the concepts surrounding a law, the practice is open to expansion (as in these examples) or limitation. It is the advent of new technology that allows *poskim* to translate the theory into practice.

Societal changes are similar to technological changes

In the case of *Havineinu* new technology and an evolving society do not necessarily change the ruling about the permissibility of the prayer. Rather, they put into question the extent to which the purpose behind the prayer can be achieved. While allowing for the continued use of *Havineinu* in contemporary times, Iggrot Moshe does not advise its use, as he sees no benefit in it.

שו"ת אגרות משה חלק או"ח ד סימן צא
אף בתפלת הבינינו שבדרך רשאי גם בזמננו, אבל כיון שלא רגיל בהבינינו ואינו בקי בה לא ירויח אלא משהו ואולי לא ירויח כלל.
Iggrot Moshe, Orach Chaim 4:91(2)
...*Havineinu* is still permitted to travelers nowadays, but since one is not used to saying *Havineinu* and not expert in it, one gains very little by saying it, perhaps nothing at all!

Within the case of *Havineinu*, the changing reality forces *poskim* to confront an interesting and difficult dilemma. As Tosafot observe, the practice of reciting *Havineinu* should only be preserved within communities which have a familiarity with it. As Iggrot Moshe states, few communities today are proficient in, let alone familiar with, this prayer. This consideration would suggest that *Havineinu* is no longer an acceptable prayer alternative. Yet, on the other hand, *Havineinu*'s purpose, also noted in Tosafot, is to allow for prayer even in the pressured situation of relative danger. While the type of daily danger experienced in the times of the Gemara is no longer a daily reality for most people, soldiers in the Israeli army do confront danger on a regular basis.

הצבא כהלכה, הלכות מלחמה וצבא פרק מ"ג

בשעת דחק גדולה, אפשר להתפלל "שמונה עשרה" בנוסח "ברכת הביננו" (כגון שהוא בדרך, או שהיה עומד במקום שהוא טרוד וירא שיפסיקוהו, או שלא יוכל להתפלל בכוונה תפילה ארוכה), גם בימות הגשמים ומוצאי שבת

HaTzava KaHalacha, Hilchot Milchamah veTzava Ch. 43
In cases of great pressing need one may recite *Shemoneh Esreh* with the text of *Havineinu* (for example, if one is traveling, or one is standing in a place where one is encumbered and afraid of being interrupted, or one is unable to direct one's intention for a full-length prayer), even during the rainy season or at the conclusion of Shabbat.

Halacha's dynamic element is a result of it being a living, applied law system. While innovations occur in the realm of study, applications of rulings to an ever-evolving reality produce change as well. When new situations come up, the logic behind a ruling must be extended to include the new situation. Because he was writing about a new phenomenon, the danger posed to the Israeli Army, HaTzava KaHalacha wrote in a footnote commenting on the above law,

הצבא כהלכה, הלכות מלחמה וצבא פרק מג

26. אף שב"ביאור הלכה" (ד"ה "או") כתב שהיום אין נוהגים להתפלל "הביננו". אין הדבר מוסכם ופסוק, ומשאר פוסקים לא משמע הכי.

HaTzava KaHalacha, Hilchot Milchamah veTzava Ch. 43
26. Even though Bi'ur Halacha (s.v. *oh*) wrote that nowadays the practice is not to say *Havineinu*, the matter is not universally agreed to or set; and the other decisors do not seem to imply this.

It should not be understood that by ruling differently than Bi'ur Halacha, HaTzava KaHalacha is putting forth an illegitimate distinction, or that he is changing the rules of *Havineinu*. Rather, he is relying on a wealth of other authorities who permit *Havineinu* in a wide variety of situations, and he convincingly argues that the dangers and pressures of army service in Israel today constitute pressing need. As he continues in his footnote, many sources—both classic and contemporary—including Kessef Mishneh, Rabbeinu Manoach, Magen Avraham, Meorot, Michtam, Siddur Tachlael, Rabbi Serayah Deblitzky and Gesher HaChaim support the contention that insertions may be made in *Havieninu* if one is certain that one will not err, leading HaTzava KaHalacha to permit soldiers to recite *Havineinu* year-round. Thus, although the driving force behind *chiddushim* that come as a result of changes in reality are based on extra-halachic sources, the means of change are faithful to the halachic process of study, thorough understanding, and correct application of the texts.

5.4 A survey of the range of opinions about Havineinu

While this section emphasizes differences in the halacha, this perspective should not overshadow the similarities between *poskim*. Universally, *Shemoneh Esreh* is viewed as the primary prayer, and its recitation ought to be upheld. All commentaries recognize that *Havineinu* was instituted as an abridgement with a specific purpose—to enable one to fulfill one's obligation of prayer when there is little alternative. With these shared premises, each commentator approaches the topic of *Havineinu* in his own unique way, offering the understanding that strikes him as most true.

Much of the analysis in this chapter has dealt with changes in understanding and application. Although briefly touched upon, there has not been a solid focus on how *chiddush* influences practical ruling. It is evident that a change has occurred in *Havineinu*'s frequency of use and in Jewish communities' overall familiarity with this prayer. There are a wide range of opinions on several aspects of *Havineinu*'s use: the factors that allow it to be recited, whether the need to recite *Havdalah* and *she'elat geshamim* hinders the use of this prayer, and whether this prayer is applicable to today's environment.

The wide range of interpretations concerning the recitation of *Havineinu* at the conclusion of Shabbat and festivals and during the rainy season is evidence of *chiddush*. The rulings range from an absolute prohibition on reciting *Havineinu* at the conclusion of Shabbat and festivals and during the rainy season—essentially half the year—to the blanket permission to recite *Havineinu* within all cases of *dechak*. Some commentaries' opinions fall in the middle ground as well, allowing the recitation of *Havineinu* at the conclusion of Shabbat and festivals, but not during the rainy season.

Even in contexts where reciting *Havineinu* is seen as an acceptable alternative to reciting *Shemoneh Esreh*, there are many opinions as to what factors allow one to recite the prayer. Bach, in interpreting Rabbi Yehoshua's opinion, claims that some opinions hold that in all situations recitation of *Havineinu* is optional, but in certain cases its recitation is obligatory. Other opinions allow recitation of *Havineinu* when *Shemoneh Esreh* is not possible—such as danger situations, *sha'at ha-dechak*, *tirdah*, lack of proficiency, lack of familiarity, and lack of time. Others point to a different goal of *Havineinu*—to preserve concentration—and claim that it can only be said when one's ability to maintain *kavvanah* is hampered. Although *sha'at ha-dechak* had been portrayed as the underlying reason in all of these approaches, some opinions, including Chayei Adam and Gesher HaChaim, even allow *Havineinu*'s recitation in situations, such as illness, that seem not to fully qualify as "*dechak*." A certain reading of the Gemara could even yield the conclusion that *Havineinu* is a suitable prayer to be used to avoid theft from an employer.

5.5 What changes with *Chiddush*?

Following the observations that *chiddush* influences practice, a fundamental question—perhaps *the* fundamental question— remains: to what extent does *chiddush* cause changes in law? What does it mean to "change" in halacha? All the developments discussed in this paper might ultimately result in a change of practice, but never without a change in law. Recognizing that maintaining fidelity to the tradition is a goal, while simultaneously acknowledging elements of *chiddush*, is not a contradictory stance. Whether approaching the text in an innovative way, or incorporating circumstantial changes, it is the applications and understandings, not the substance of the law, that change.

Ultimately, Jewish law's evolution—the incremental change in practice that anyone who has studied halacha clearly sees—is a result of incremental innovation caused by the interplay of changing realities.

First, there is sincere Torah study: as one studies the Mishnah and Talmud, the commentaries and codes, one sometimes understands the sources differently from those in previous generations. We might be dwarfs, but we are privileged to stand on the shoulders of giants, as Razah (R. Zerachiah HaLevi, also known as Ba'al HaMaor for his illuminating commentaries on the Rif) notes, and we see differently and sometimes more (or farther) than our predecessors.

Sometimes technology and sociology change, and thus applying the basic principles formed in the Talmud to a later time requires innovative application of the halachic texts. Prayer in an ancient, dangerous, and bookless society is quite different from prayer in a modern, safe, and text-rich place. As we observed earlier, the needs of a situation often call for revisiting the corpus of Jewish law texts, honestly analyzing and interpreting the sources, and perhaps reviving a dormant line of thinking within the tradition— an opinion or opinions that may once again prove relevant. That is the essence of innovation in Jewish law.

Appendices
Havineinu texts

Appendix A
Text of *Havineinu* according to the Babylonian Talmud (Berachot 29a)

הֲבִינֵנוּ ה' אֱ-לֹהֵינוּ לָדַעַת דְּרָכֶיךָ, וּמוֹל אֶת לְבָבֵנוּ לְיִרְאָתֶךָ, וְתִסְלַח לָנוּ
לִהְיוֹת גְּאוּלִים, וְרַחֲקֵנוּ מִמַּכְאוֹבֵינוּ, וְדַשְּׁנֵנוּ בִּנְאוֹת אַרְצֶךָ, וּנְפוּצוֹתֵינוּ
מֵאַרְבַּע תְּקַבֵּץ, וְהַתּוֹעִים עַל דַּעְתְּךָ יִשָּׁפֵטוּ, וְעַל הָרְשָׁעִים תָּנִיף יָדֶךָ,
וְיִשְׂמְחוּ צַדִּיקִים בְּבִנְיַן עִירֶךָ וּבְתִקּוּן הֵיכָלֶךָ וּבִצְמִיחַת קֶרֶן לְדָוִד עַבְדֶּךָ
וּבַעֲרִיכַת נֵר לְבֶן יִשַׁי מְשִׁיחֶךָ, טֶרֶם נִקְרָא אַתָּה תַעֲנֶה. בָּרוּךְ אַתָּה ה',
שׁוֹמֵעַ תְּפִלָּה.

Grant us, Lord, our God, wisdom to understand Your ways; subject our hearts to worship You; forgive us so that we may be redeemed; keep us from suffering; satisfy us with the products of Your earth; gather our dispersed people from the four corners of the earth. Judge those who stray from Your path; punish the wicked; may the righteous rejoice over the building of Your city, the restoration of Your temple, the flourishing dynasty of Your servant David, and the continuation of the offspring of Your anointed, the son of Jesse. Answer us before You call. Blessed are You, O Lord, who hears prayers.

Appendix B
Text of *Havineinu* according to the Jerusalem Talmud (Berachot 4:3)

הֲבִינֵנוּ רְצֵה תְשׁוּבָתֵינוּ סְלַח לָנוּ גּוֹאֲלֵנוּ רַפֵּא חֲלָיֵינוּ בָּרֵךְ שְׁנוֹתֵינוּ –
...אִם הָיוּ גְּשָׁמִים אוֹמְרִים גִּשְׁמֵי בְרָכָה, אִם הָיוּ טְלָלִים אוֹמְרִים בְּטַלְלֵי
בְרָכָה – כִּי מְפוּזָרִים אַתָּה מְקַבֵּץ וְתוֹעִין עָלֶיךָ לִשְׁפּוֹט וְעַל הָרְשָׁעִים
תָּשִׁית יָדָךְ וְיִשְׂמְחוּ כָּל חוֹסֵי בָךְ בְּבִנְיַן עִירָךְ וּבְחִידוּשׁ בֵּית מִקְדָּשָׁךְ
וּבְצֶמַח דָּוִד עַבְדָּךְ כִּי טֶרֶם נִקְרָא אַתָּה תַעֲנֶה כָּאָמוּר וְהָיָה טֶרֶם יִקְרָאוּ וַאֲנִי
אֶעֱנֶה עוֹד הֵם מְדַבְּרִים וַאֲנִי אֶשְׁמָע, בָּרוּךְ אַתָּה ה' שׁוֹמֵעַ תְּפִלָּה. וְאוֹמֵר
שָׁלוֹשׁ בְּרָכוֹת רִאשׁוֹנוֹת וְשָׁלוֹשׁ בְּרָכוֹת אַחֲרוֹנוֹת. וְאוֹמֵר בָּרוּךְ ה' כִּי שָׁמַע
קוֹל תַּחֲנוּנָי.

Grant us wisdom, accept our repentance, forgive us Our Redeemer, heal our sick, bless our years—... in the rainy season one says, [with] rains of blessing; in the summer season one says, with dews of blessing—for You are the ingatherer of the scattered, You will judge those who stray, You will stretch Your hand against the wicked, those who take shelter in You will rejoice in the rebuilding of Your city and the rededication of Your temple and the restoration of the line of Your servant David, for before we call out You answer, as it is written: "And it shall come to pass that, before they call, I will answer, and while they are yet speaking, I will hear" (Isa. 65:24). Blessed are You, O Lord, who hears prayers. One says the first three blessings and the last three blessings, and one says "Blessed is the Lord, for He has heard the voice of my supplications" (Ps. 28:6).

Appendix C
Text of *Havineinu* with additions for the conclusion of Shabbat and Festivals and for the rainy season as per the view of R. Akiva Eiger, Gesher HaChaim, and HaTzava KaHalacha

הֲבִינֵנוּ ה' אֱ-לֹהֵינוּ [בְּמוֹצָאֵי שַׁבָּת קוֹדֶשׁ וּבְמוֹצָאֵי יוֹם-טוֹב מוֹסִיף: הַמַּבְדִּיל בֵּין קוֹדֶשׁ לְחוֹל] לָדַעַת דְּרָכֶיךָ, וּמוֹל אֶת לְבָבֵנוּ לְיִרְאָתֶךָ, וְתִסְלַח לָנוּ לִהְיוֹת גְּאוּלִים, וְרַחֲקֵנוּ מִמַּכְאוֹב, וְדַשְּׁנֵנוּ בִּנְאוֹת אַרְצֶךָ [בַּחוֹרֶף מוֹסִיף: וְתֵן טַל וּמָטָר], וּנְפוּצוֹתֵינוּ מֵאַרְבַּע (כַּנְפוֹת הָאָרֶץ) תְּקַבֵּץ, וְהַתּוֹעִים עַל דַּעְתְּךָ יִשָּׁפֵטוּ, וְעַל הָרְשָׁעִים תָּנִיף יָדֶךָ, וְיִשְׂמְחוּ צַדִּיקִים בְּבִנְיַן עִירֶךָ וּבְתִקּוּן הֵיכָלֶךָ וּבִצְמִיחַת קֶרֶן לְדָוִד עַבְדֶּךָ וַעֲרִיכַת נֵר לְבֶן יִשַׁי מְשִׁיחֶךָ, טֶרֶם נִקְרָא אַתָּה תַעֲנֶה. בָּרוּךְ אַתָּה ה', שׁוֹמֵעַ תְּפִלָּה.

Grant us, Lord, our God, [*at the conclusion of Shabbat and Festivals one adds:* the One who distinguishes between holy and profane,] wisdom to understand Your ways; subject our hearts to worship You; forgive us so that we may be redeemed; keep us from suffering; satisfy us with the products of Your earth [*during the rainy season one adds:* and send dew and rain]; gather our dispersed people from the four (corners of the earth). Judge those who stray from Your path; punish the wicked; may the righteous rejoice over the building of Your city, the restoration of Your temple, the flourishing dynasty of Your servant David, and the continuation of the offspring of Your anointed, the son of Jesse. Answer us before You call. Blessed are You, O Lord, who hears prayers.

Appendix D
Text of *Me'ein Shemoneh Esreh* (Rav's version) according to Chayei Adam

יֹאמַר תְּחִלָּה ג' רִאשׁוֹנוֹת כְּדַרְכּוֹ וְאַחַר כַּךְ בְּמוֹצָאֵי שַׁבָּת יֹאמַר, אַתָּה חוֹנַנְתָּנוּ לְמַדַּע תּוֹרָתֶךָ, וַתַּבְדִּילֵנוּ ה' אֱ-לֹהֵינוּ בֵּין קוֹדֶשׁ לְחוֹל, בֵּין אוֹר לְחשֶׁךְ, בֵּין יִשְׂרָאֵל לָעַמִּים, בֵּין יוֹם הַשְּׁבִיעִי לְשֵׁשֶׁת יְמֵי הַמַּעֲשֶׂה, וְחָנֵּנוּ מֵאִתָּךְ כו'. וּבְחוֹל יֹאמַר אַתָּה חוֹנֵן לְאָדָם דַּעַת, חָנֵּנוּ מֵאִתָּךְ דֵּעָה בִּינָה וְהַשְׂכֵּל. בָּרוּךְ אַתָּה ה' חוֹנֵן הַדָּעַת. הֲשִׁיבֵנוּ אָבִינוּ לְתוֹרָתֶךָ, וְהַחֲזִירֵנוּ בִּתְשׁוּבָה שְׁלֵמָה לְפָנֶיךָ. בָּרוּךְ אַתָּה ה', הָרוֹצֶה בִּתְשׁוּבָה. סְלַח לָנוּ אָבִינוּ, כִּי מוֹחֵל וְסוֹלֵחַ אָתָּה. בָּרוּךְ אַתָּה ה', חַנּוּן הַמַּרְבֶּה לִסְלֹחַ. רְאֵה נָא בְעָנְיֵנוּ וּגְאָלֵנוּ מְהֵרָה, כִּי גוֹאֵל חָזָק אָתָּה. בא"י גּוֹאֵל יִשְׂרָאֵל. רְפָאֵנוּ ה' וְנֵרָפֵא, כִּי אֵ-ל מֶלֶךְ רוֹפֵא נֶאֱמָן אָתָּה. בא"י רוֹפֵא חוֹלֵי עַמּוֹ יִשְׂרָאֵל. בָּרֵךְ עָלֵינוּ אֶת הַשָּׁנָה הַזֹּאת, וְתֵן טַל וּמָטָר לִבְרָכָה עַל פְּנֵי הָאֲדָמָה, וּבָרֵךְ שְׁנָתֵנוּ כַּשָּׁנִים הַטּוֹבוֹת. בא"י מְבָרֵךְ הַשָּׁנִים. תְּקַע בְּשׁוֹפָר גָּדוֹל לְחֵרוּתֵנוּ, וְקַבְּצֵנוּ יַחַד מֵאַרְבַּע כַּנְפוֹת הָאָרֶץ. בא"י מְקַבֵּץ נִדְחֵי עַמּוֹ יִשְׂרָאֵל. הָשִׁיבָה שׁוֹפְטֵינוּ כְּבָרִאשׁוֹנָה, וּמְלוֹךְ עָלֵינוּ אַתָּה ה' לְבַדֶּךָ, וְצַדְּקֵנוּ בַּמִּשְׁפָּט. בא"י מֶלֶךְ אוֹהֵב צְדָקָה וּמִשְׁפָּט. וְלַמַּלְשִׁינִים אַל תְּהִי תִקְוָה, וְכָל אוֹיְבֶיךָ מְהֵרָה יִכָּרֵתוּ, וְתַכְנִיעֵם בִּמְהֵרָה בְיָמֵינוּ. בא"י שׁוֹבֵר אוֹיְבִים וּמַכְנִיעַ זֵדִים. עַל הַצַּדִּיקִים וְעַל הַחֲסִידִים וְעָלֵינוּ יֶהֱמוּ רַחֲמֶיךָ, וְשִׂים חֶלְקֵנוּ עִמָּהֶם לְעוֹלָם וְלֹא נֵבוֹשׁ, כִּי בְךָ בָּטַחְנוּ. בא"י מִשְׁעָן וּמִבְטָח לַצַּדִּיקִים. וְלִירוּשָׁלַיִם עִירְךָ בְּרַחֲמִים תָּשׁוּב, וּבְנֵה אוֹתָהּ בְּקָרוֹב, וְכִסֵּא דָוִד מְהֵרָה לְתוֹכָהּ תָּכִין. בא"י בּוֹנֵה יְרוּשָׁלָיִם. אֶת צֶמַח דָּוִד עַבְדְּךָ מְהֵרָה תַצְמִיחַ, כִּי לִישׁוּעָתְךָ קִוִּינוּ כָּל הַיּוֹם. בא"י מַצְמִיחַ קֶרֶן יְשׁוּעָה. שְׁמַע קוֹלֵנוּ וְקַבֵּל בְּרַחֲמִים וּבְרָצוֹן אֶת תְּפִלָּתֵנוּ, כִּי אֵ-ל שׁוֹמֵעַ תְּפִלּוֹת אָתָּה, בא"י שׁוֹמֵעַ תְּפִלָּה. וְאַחַר כַּךְ אוֹמֵר ג' אַחֲרוֹנוֹת וּמְסַיֵּם הַמְבָרֵךְ אֶת עַמּוֹ יִשְׂרָאֵל בַּשָּׁלוֹם. יִהְיוּ לְרָצוֹן כו' עוֹשֶׂה שָׁלוֹם כו':

One first recites the first three blessings as usual, and then at the conclusion of Shabbat one says, "You have graciously endowed us with a knowledge of Your Torah, and have made a distinction for us, O Lord our God, between sacred and profane, between light and darkness, between Israel and other nations, between the seventh day and the six days of work, and graciously endow us, etc." During the week one says, "You graciously grant humans knowledge, graciously endow us with knowledge, wisdom and discernment from You; Blessed are You, O Lord, gracious giver of knowledge. Return us, our Father, to Your Torah, and bring us back in complete repentance before You; Blessed are You, O Lord, who desires repentance. Forgive us, our Father, for You are one to pardon and forgive; Blessed are You, O Lord, who is gracious and abundantly forgives. Look, please, at our affliction, and speedily redeem us, for You are a mighty redeemer; Blessed are You, O Lord, redeemer of Israel. Heal us, O Lord, and we shall be healed, for You are an almighty king and faithful healer; blessed are You, O Lord, healer of the sick of His people Israel. Bless this year for us, and send dew and rain as a blessing upon the face of the earth, and bless our year as the other good years; Blessed are You, O Lord, who blesses the years. Blow a great shofar to proclaim our freedom, and gather us together from the four corners of the earth; Blessed are You, O Lord, who gathers the dispersed of Your people Israel. Restore our judges as in earlier times, and reign over us, O Lord, solely, and defend us in judgment; Blessed are You, O Lord, the king who loves righteousness and judgment. And for slanderers let there be no hope, and may all Your enemies be speedily cut off, and may they be brought low speedily in our time; Blessed are You, O Lord, who destroys enemies and lowers the wicked. Upon the righteous and upon the pious and upon us may Your mercy be aroused, and set our share with them forever, so that we shall not be put to shame, for we have trusted in You; Blessed are You, O Lord, the support and haven of the righteous. And to Jerusalem Your city may You mercifully return, and rebuild it soon, and speedily prepare the throne of David; Blessed are You, O Lord, who rebuilds Jerusalem. May You speedily cause the offshoot of Your servant David to flourish, for we have waited for Your salvation all the day; Blessed are You, O Lord, who causes the rays of salvation to flourish. Hear our voices and mercifully and willingly accept our prayers, for You are a God who hears prayers; Blessed are You, O Lord, who hears prayers." Afterward, one says the last three blessings and concludes with, "Who blesses his nation Israel with peace." "Let [the words of my mouth] be acceptable, etc." "The One who makes peace on high, etc."

Index

About the Author

MICHAEL J. BROYDE is a full professor at Emory University School of Law and a Senior Fellow and Project Director at the Center for the Study of Law and Religion at Emory University. His primary areas of interest are Jewish law and ethics, law and religion, and comparative religious law. Besides Jewish law and family law, Prof. Broyde has taught Federal Courts, Alternative Dispute Resolution, Secured Credit, Bankruptcy, and other courses. He received his JD from New York University in 1988 and published a note on the *Law Review*. A year later, he clerked for Judge Leonard I. Garth of the United States Court of Appeals, Third Circuit.

Prof. Broyde was ordained *(yoreh yoreh ve-yadin yadin)* by Yeshiva University's Rabbi Isaac Elchanan Theological Seminary and is a member *(chaver)* of the Beth Din of America, the largest Jewish law court in America (affiliated with the Rabbinical Council of America). During the 1997–98 academic year, Rabbi Broyde was the Director of the Beth Din while on leave from Emory University. In addition, he was the founding rabbi of the Young Israel of Toco Hills in Atlanta, Ga., and for many years delivered a daily advanced halacha (Jewish law) class to the members of the Atlanta Torah MiTzion kollel.

Yeshiva University Review has called Prof. Broyde "the most prolific scholar of comparative law and Halakhah working in the United States today, and is considered by many to have done the best work." He has published more than seventy-five articles and book chapters on various aspects of law and religion and Jewish law, including "A Jewish View of World Law," *Emory Law Journal* 54:79–93 (spec. ed., 2005) about how Jewish law might classify international law, and a series of vigorous exchanges in several publications on military ethics in Jewish law. He is a regular contributor to *The Journal of Halacha and Contemporary Society,*

Tehumin, Tradition: A Journal of Jewish Thought, and *The Jewish Law Annual,* and has had editorials published in a wide array of newspapers, from the *New York Times* and the *International Herald Tribune* to the *Jewish Week* and the *Jewish Press.*

Prof. Broyde has authored and edited several volumes: *Human Rights in Judaism* (Jason Aronson, 1997), *Marriage, Divorce and the Abandoned Wife in Jewish Law: A Conceptual Understanding of the Agunah Problems in America* (Ktav, 2001), and *Marriage, Sex, and Family in Judaism* (Rowman & Littlefield, 2005). A second, revised edition of his first book, *The Pursuit of Justice and Jewish Law* (Yeshiva University Press, 1996), was published by Yashar Books (2007).